Rigoberta Menchú Tum

Activist for Indigenous Rights in Guatemala

MODERN PEACEMAKERS

Modern Peacemakers

Rigoberta Menchú Tum

Activist for Indigenous Rights in Guatemala

Heather Lehr Wagner

CHELSEA HOUSE
PUBLISHERS
An imprint of Infobase Publishing

Rigoberta Menchú Tum

Copyright © 2007 by Infobase Publishing

Chelsea House
An imprint of Infobase Publishing
132 West 31st Street
New York, NY 10001

ISBN-10: 0-7910-8998-3
ISBN-13: 978-0-7910-8998-9

Library of Congress Cataloging-in-Publication Data

Wagner, Heather Lehr.
   Rigoberta Menchú Tum : activist for indigenous rights in Guatemala / Heather Lehr Wagner.
      p. cm. — (Modern peacemakers)
   Includes bibliographical references and index.
   ISBN 0-7910-8998-3 (hardcover)
   1. Menchú, Rigoberta—Juvenile literature. 2. Quiché women—Biography—Juvenile literature. 3. Women human rights workers—Guatemala—Biography—Juvenile literature. 4. Mayas —Guatemala—Government relations—Juvenile literature. I. Title. II. Series.
   F1465.2.Q5W34 2007
   972.81004'97415—dc22
   [B]   2006028382

Text design by Annie O'Donnell
Cover design by Takeshi Takahashi

Printed in the United States of America
Bang FOF 10 9 8 7 6 5 4 3 2 1

This book is printed on acid-free paper.

TABLE OF CONTENTS

CHAPTER 1

Life and Peace

O n the night of October 13, 1992, activist Rigoberta Menchú was sleeping in the diocesan headquarters of the Catholic Church in San Mareos, a town in western Guatemala, near the Mexican border. She was 33 years old and a member of a poor Mayan peasant family. From the time she was a teenager, she had campaigned tirelessly against the discrimination her people suffered at the hands of the Guatemalan government and its wealthiest landowners.

When Menchú was growing up, her family spent several months each year working on large coffee plantations, picking coffee beans for long hours each day. Despite the grueling labor, the family barely made enough to survive. By the time Menchú reached adulthood, most of her family had become involved in the struggle to achieve better living and working conditions for Guatemala's indigenous (native) population. At one point, her father was accused of having been involved in the murder of a plantation owner, so he was arrested and tortured. He would later be killed. Menchú's mother and brother were also arrested, tortured, and killed by the Guatemalan army.

Rigoberta Menchú Tum walks with other Mayans in a demonstration against oppression in Sololá, Guatemala. Menchú took part in many such demonstrations, including one in San Mareos, which took place just before Menchú was informed that she had won the Nobel Peace Prize.

The murder of her beloved family members inspired Menchú to become a voice for those who had no voice. She became an outspoken critic of the government, sharing her testimony of what had happened to her family and encouraging others to resist and combat the Guatemalan military. As a result, she was threatened by the government, forced to hide and then flee to Mexico, where she was able to organize international pressure on the Guatemalan government. The needs of her "brothers and sisters," as she called other indigenous Guatemalans, drew her back to Guatemala eventually.

On that October night in San Mareos, Menchú was resting. Earlier, she had participated in a demonstration attended by laborers, peasants, and the people who worked on sugarcane, coffee, and banana plantations. The local governor had refused to provide microphones or a public building for the rally, so the demonstrators instead filled the streets.

Menchú had planned to stay at a boardinghouse in San Mareos, but when her plans were discovered, the proprietor received threats. She searched for another safe haven and finally found one in the local Catholic church. The larger organization had supported her work in the past. That night, the priest in San Mareos granted Menchú the use of his office in the diocese head-quarters. There, she talked for a while with the men and women who were traveling with her, then she tried to get some sleep.

Menchú had been asleep for several hours when the ringing of a telephone awakened her. On the other end of the telephone line, a man identified himself as the Norwegian ambassador to Mexico. "In nine minutes," the ambassador said, "it will be announced that you have won the Nobel Peace Prize. Let me be the first to congratulate you. You have nine minutes to prepare yourself; after that, the news will be out."

Dazed, Menchú asked him to confirm what he had said.

"I am the Norwegian ambassador in Mexico," he replied. "It is my job to give you the news."[1]

Menchú was stunned. She hung up the phone, uncertain what to do next. Her travel companions asked her what had happened.

"We've got the Nobel Prize," she replied.[2]

Those traveling with Menchú cried. The priest at the church set off fireworks and rang the church bells. Rigoberta Menchú's thoughts quickly turned to her parents, though—to her father and mother, who had suffered torture and been murdered, fight-ing for the very cause that had now brought their daughter the highest international acclaim.

In her first press conference, only minutes after she learned that she had been chosen to receive the Nobel Peace Prize, Menchú's words were simple and few: "How I would love to have all my family alive and here with me," she said. "Because life is peace. I desire life and peace."[3]

A MAYAN WOMAN

Rigoberta Menchú's family formed the core of her struggle for justice. Her impoverished childhood exposed her to the brutal inequalities in Guatemala and to the prejudice exercised against the native Indian population. Menchú was immersed in her native Mayan-K'iche' culture and was fiercely protective of its uniqueness and beauty.

As a result of her activism, however, Menchú's definition of *family* had broadened, first to include all members of her K'iche' tribe, then to include all indigenous Guatemalan people.

History of the Nobel Peace Prize

The awarding of an annual Prize for Peace was the idea of the scientist and inventor Alfred Nobel, who was born in Stockholm, Sweden, on October 21, 1833. When Nobel died in 1896, his will specified that a significant portion of his fortune should be dedicated to the creation of five prizes, including one for peace. Nobel stipulated that the peace prize be given to the person who had done "the most or best work for fraternity between nations, for the abolition or reduction of standing armies, and for the holding of peace congresses." Nobel also specified that, unlike the other prizes, which were to be awarded by Swedish committees, the prize for peace was to be awarded by a committee of five people elected by the Norwegian *Storting* (parliament).

The first Nobel Peace Prize was awarded in 1901 to joint recipients Frédéric Passy and Jean Henry Dunant. Passy was leader of the French peace movement and main organizer of the first Universal Peace Congress. Dunant was the founder of the International Red Cross.

Over the years, the Nobel Peace Prize has been awarded to both organizations and individuals. The first recipient organization was the Institute for International Law, honored in 1904 for its efforts to come up with the general principles that would form the science

Eventually, all those who supported the campaign for human rights would be called her "brothers and sisters."

Menchú, in her autobiography *I, Rigoberta Menchú*, recounted in straightforward prose the early years of her life. She revealed the cruel conditions and injustice experienced by the indigenous population of Guatemala. The book depicted ordinary life for Menchú and her family, but it was an ordinary life marked by loss and suffering, struggle and abuse. As she noted at the beginning of her autobiography, "My story is the story of all poor Guatemalans. My personal experience is the reality of a whole people."[4]

of international law. The International Committee of the Red Cross received the prize twice—in 1917 and 1944, for its efforts to promote international solidarity and brotherhood in the midst of war. The Office of the United Nations High Commissioner for Refugees received the prize in 1954; other organizations to receive the prize include the United Nations Children's Fund (UNICEF) in 1965, the Friends Service Council in Britain/American Friends Service Committee (1947), United Nations Peacekeeping Forces (1988), International Physicians for the Prevention of Nuclear War (1985), and Médécins sans Frontières (Doctors Without Borders) in 1999.

Over the years, the award has highlighted the achievements of men and women from many different nations who represent widely varying backgrounds and experiences. It is interesting to note that one of the people most closely identified with nonviolence, Mohandas Gandhi of India, never received the Nobel Peace Prize, despite five nominations. Rigoberta Menchú is one of only 12 women to receive the Nobel Prize—a group that also includes Bertha von Suttner (1905), Jane Addams (1931), Emily Greene Balch (1946), Betty Williams and Mairead Corrigan (1976), Mother Teresa (1979), Alva Myrdal (1982), Aung San Suu Kyi (1991), Jody Williams (1997), Shirin Ebadi (2003), and Wangari Maathai (2004).

Rigoberta Menchú answers questions during a news conference at California State University, Fresno, on November 18, 2003. Since being awarded the Nobel Prize, Menchú has been invited to speak throughout the world.

Through this simple and moving testimony and through her tireless campaign for human rights in her native land, Menchú moved from peasant to national heroine. In the presentation speech for the 1992 Nobel Peace Prize, Francis Sejersted, chairperson of the Norwegian Nobel Committee, said, "By maintaining a disarming humanity in a brutal world, Rigoberta Menchú Tum appeals to the best in all of us, wherever we live and whatever our background. She stands as a uniquely potent symbol of a just struggle."[5]

CHAPTER 2

Childhood in the Mountains

In her autobiography *I, Rigoberta Menchú,* the future Nobel laureate described the customs of the Mayan-K'iche' community to which she belonged—tales of traditions that shaped her earliest memories and the woman she would become. In Menchú's account, she referred to her native community as *Quiché.* In recent years, the spelling of this native Guatemalan group was changed to K'iche', and so we will use the contemporary spelling in this book. "Quiché" continues to be used, however, to refer both to the department (or state) of Guatemala where Menchú was born, and in some cases for the dialect she and her people speak.

When a child is born into a family of K'iche' Mayans, he or she belongs to the community. This sense of community involvement in the life of each new child is demonstrated before that child's birth.

Within each K'iche' community are elected leaders—a man and a woman who are chosen by the people to serve as mother and father to the community. When a couple learns that they are expecting a baby, they go to the community leaders to tell them of their pregnancy. The leaders then pledge the support of the community: They

Mayan Indians carry water back to their house in Santiago Atitlán, Guatemala. The traditional methods of day-to-day tasks have been preserved in many Mayan communities, including the K'iche' community into which Rigoberta Menchú was born.

agree to serve as "grandparents" to the child, then help the couple choose godparents to help raise the unborn baby.

Each day of her pregnancy, the mother-to-be is visited by neighbors, who bring her small gifts. In the seventh month, the K'iche' mother introduces her baby to the life he or she will lead. She takes walks outdoors and follows her usual work routine so that the baby will become accustomed to the habits of the family, whether that means getting up early to do chores, working in the fields, or caring for animals. She also talks constantly to her unborn child: explaining the tasks she is performing, giving instructions, and offering advice.

The husband is present at the baby's birth, as are three couples—the village leaders and both sets of the couple's parents. Other children are kept away. The newborn baby stays alone with the mother for eight days. Neighbors bring food for the mother and presents for the baby, but the two are largely left alone to slowly introduce the baby to his or her new world.

At the end of the eighth day, the family counts the number of people who brought food for the mother and gifts for the baby. These gifts might include eggs or other food, clothing, animals, firewood, or the offer of help to carry water or chop wood. If most of the community has provided something during the eight days, this is a great honor and means that the child must be responsible for the community when he or she grows older.

Rigoberta Menchú's family followed these customs when she was born. After eight days, she and her mother were washed and dressed in clean clothes. The whole house was cleaned, and mother and baby were placed in a bed made with fresh, clean sheets. Four candles were placed on the corners of the bed to represent the four corners of the child's new home and the respect the child must have toward her community. The candles were lit, and they gave off incense.

Finally, Rigoberta was ready to enter her new world. A party was held when she was born; a second party was held after eight days. Neighbors brought food, and lunch was provided at the Menchús' home for the whole community. The baby's brothers, sisters, family, and friends were finally allowed to see her, and to hug and kiss her.

It is K'iche' custom for the parents of the baby to publicly tell her of the difficulties she will be facing. They tell her of how the family has suffered. They tell her how hard her life will be. They tell her of their sadness at bringing a child into the world to struggle and suffer. Then they tell her that she must be responsible for her community and honor its customs and rules. After this, everyone eats lunch together, and the neighbors return to their homes.

The importance of community is also stressed at the child's baptism, which happens when she is 40 days old. On this day, the child officially becomes a member of the community. Important

people from the village make speeches. They promise to be responsible for the child and to teach her the K'iche' ways. The parents
promise to teach the child to respect K'iche' traditions. The names
of K'iche' ancestors are recited, and the child is reminded of her
responsibility to all those who have gone before her.

BORN TO RESPONSIBILITY

This sense of commitment to the community was made clear to
Rigoberta Menchú from the time of her birth on January 9, 1959.
She was the sixth child of Vicente Menchú and Juana Tum Cotojá,
who had formed their own community in Chimel, in the mountains of central Guatemala. They cleared and cultivated the land,
and planted the corn that forms the staple of the K'iche' diet.

Rigoberta and her family were K'iche', which means they
belonged to one of the groups of Mayan and native Guatemalans
who make up about 40 percent of Guatemala's population of 12
million. Most of the rest of the population are descendants of the
Spaniards who arrived in Central America and conquered the
Mayan kingdoms there in the sixteenth century. They are called
ladinos, a term that refers to their European or mixed descent.
Strong racial and ethnic prejudices exist between the Indians and
the ladinos, and at the time of Rigoberta's birth, it was the ladinos
who were firmly in control of Guatemala.

Not all Indians living in Guatemala are K'iche'. In fact, the
K'iche' make up little more than 9 percent of Guatemala's population. Twenty-three different indigenous languages are spoken
in Guatemala. The native population includes Kaqchikel, Mam,
Q'eqchi, and other Mayan and non-Mayan indigenous people. It
was not until she was older that Rigoberta learned Spanish, the
language of the ladinos, which was considered a tool to communicate with those in power.

Rigoberta's father, Vicente Menchú, was born into poverty.
His father died when he was very young, and he and his younger
brothers moved with their mother to Uspantán, a region in the

Quiché department, to work as servants for a wealthy ladino family. Vicente was eventually sent away to live with another family, who raised him and taught him to work in the fields.

Vicente served in the army and worked briefly as a deliverer of legal documents before marrying Juana Tum Cotojá, the teenaged daughter of a relatively prosperous farmer. They had five children before Rigoberta was born; two of them died at a young age.

Vicente decided to follow his in-laws and settle a stretch of unpopulated land in the fertile mountainous region of Uspantán, in central Guatemala. Vicente and a group of homesteaders set to work, clearing the land of trees, planting corn, and building homes. Vicente built his home on a pasture near a small stream. K'iche' homes were traditionally adobe structures made of dried mud bricks, but rain fell so often in the region that the settlers decided, instead, to build their homes using wooden planks with roofs of tin or thatch.

Vicente quickly became involved in a dispute over the rights to the land he had settled. In her memoir, *I, Rigoberta Menchú,* Menchú suggests that those her father fought with were wealthy landowners, who arrived on the scene after Vicente had cultivated the land and harvested crops for several seasons.[6] Other accounts have suggested that the dispute may have been with his wife's uncle over rights to the portion of land where Vicente had built his home and planted his fields.[7] The dispute widened when Vicente invited more people to help settle the territory— the Tums felt that Vicente should have asked their permission before bringing in strangers to live on what they felt was their land.[8]

Whatever the true cause of the dispute, it is certain that for much of Rigoberta's childhood, her father was continuously struggling to hold onto his land. The family was evicted from their home at least twice, and Vicente was forced to make numerous trips to the National Institute for Agrarian Transformation (INTA), the government land office. The INTA distributed public land and settled land claims when there were conflicts.

Menchú tells of 22 separate occasions on which her father traveled by truck to the capital, Guatemala City. The INTA scheduled the appointments for a particular day and time, and there was a fine for those who failed to turn up on the scheduled day. At the age of seven, Rigoberta accompanied her father on a trip to the INTA office. She described watching her father take off his hat and give a sort of bow to the man sitting at a big table typing on a typewriter, and remembered him speaking to the people there in "a very humble way."[9]

These numerous trips made Vicente bitter toward the INTA and the government. The INTA would lose Vicente's petitions outlining his claims to the land, or state that the land had to be surveyed again and again, or simply ignore his requests. It was a humiliating reminder that in the Guatemalan system, an illiterate, indigenous farmer had very little power.

On two occasions—in 1970 and 1978—Vicente was jailed, and in one case he was beaten badly enough to be hospitalized. One of the jail sentences charged Vicente with taking apart a structure that had been built on what he felt was his land. He spent nearly 15 months in prison. In 1978, he was arrested again, and spent more than a week in jail before being bailed out by members of his community.

CHILDHOOD PARADISE

Despite her father's struggles to claim the land, Menchú's memories of her childhood in the village of Chimel—the name given to the community her father and his friends had founded—are full of happy moments. Catholic missionaries built a chapel there, and farmers raised corn and beans on the fertile land. The settlers frequently held fiestas, or celebrations, in which a neighbor would kill a pig or sheep and the whole village would be invited to the feast. Alcohol abuse had become a problem in many indigenous communities, but alcohol was forbidden in Chimel. People lived in relative peace with one another; the whole community watched over the children, and personal property was respected—there was no fear that a tool or animal left outside would be stolen.

In her memoir *Crossing Borders*, Menchú noted that she could still remember the magic of Chimel:

> My elders, my grandfather and my grandmother, my father and my mother, they have always lived there, and in my mind they still do. Chimel is a place where the clouds float lazily over the humid mountains. The colour of the mountains is dark blue, but when the sky clears, limpid and stark, it is as if the world is born anew. The colours shine, the faces of the people glow, the air is crystal clear.[10]

As an adult, Menchú kept a small bit of soil from Chimel in her garden. Her thoughts were often filled with memories of Chimel and her family life there.

Menchú remembered dreaming rich, vivid dreams as a child, and then waking and running to tell her parents what she had dreamed. It was usually her mother who would explain the meaning of the dream.

In Chimel, there was little formal education. Children, however, learned how to plant, grow crops, cook, and care for babies by working alongside their parents. Village elders taught them the Mayan customs and the meanings of different types of bird songs.

Rigoberta Menchú was born at 8:00 A.M. on January 9. Even her name indicates the class struggle in Guatemala. It is only since 1979, because of her international prominence and the publication of her first book, that she has been known as Rigoberta Menchú Tum. Her real name is "M'in"; she was named for her maternal grandmother. When her father traveled to the municipal offices to register her birth and declared his daughter's name of "M'in," however, the officials refused to register the birth. They claimed that the K'iche' name was not a "real" name. They told him that they would only register a child who was named for one of the Catholic saints.

The officials read to Rigoberta's father a list of the saints' names, and he selected Rigoberta. "I don't know why he chose it," Rigoberta later recalled. "None of my family could ever pronounce it, especially Mama. She always said 'Beta' or 'Tita.' At home, they always called me M'in."[11] (As with many Latin-American names, Rigoberta's surname, Menchú, immediately follows her given, or first, name. Her mother's maiden name, Tum, follows her surname.)

Rigoberta's mother was a healer and midwife. She helped deliver many of the babies born in Chimel. She used natural remedies to cure illnesses—plants and herbs for stomachaches, worms, hunger pains, and sore feet.

Rigoberta's parents treated their sons and daughters equally. No favoritism was shown to the sons. Every child was expected to work hard, and it was Rigoberta, not one of her brothers, who would often accompany her father whenever business took him away from the home.

Rain was a permanent feature of life in Chimel, and Rigoberta and her family often went to bed in damp clothes that had not dried by the time they awoke. The children spent hours outdoors, walking through the mud sometimes searching for mushrooms in the forest. Other times, Rigoberta and her younger brother Petrocinio would go into the hills to pick mulberries.

Young Rigoberta would climb trees if it was her job to tend the sheep. Her mother felt tree climbing was not something little girls should do, though, and if she caught her daughter up in a tree, she would smack her with a peach-tree branch.

The children would carefully watch over the beehives near their home. Bees are surrounded by many K'iche' myths, and the honey was a valuable treat, shared with neighbors and given as a gesture of friendship to people in nearby villages.

Rigoberta's father was Catholic, but her mother believed more in Mayan customs and expressions of faith. The parents solved this difference by sharing both religions with their children. They celebrated the Mayan festivals as well as the Catholic holidays, especially the Holy Week leading up to Easter.

Above, an indigenous woman washes her daughter's hair in the village of El Triunfo, Guatemala. Similarly, Rigoberta Menchú's mother taught her daughter how to perform such domestic tasks.

It was during Holy Week that the family would gather honey from their beehives and make presents of it for their neighbors. Menchú remembered Holy Week as the only time that her parents bought a large amount of flour. One of their neighbors had an oven, and it would be used to bake bread and honey cakes. For four days, neighbors would visit each other, sharing a little of what they had—honey, bread, a honey cake. The community exchanged gifts in this way. Rigoberta and her brothers and sisters would take some honey or a basket of bread to a neighbor, who would then fill their honey jar or give them bread. According to Menchú:

> We ate more in those few days than in the rest of the year put together. In the course of the morning, each neighbour would give us loads of bread and honey, and we had to eat it then and

there. We never refused, because our parents had brought us up to accept everything, to eat just enough to be polite and take the rest home. At lunchtime, people made white *tortillas*, and white beans with dried fish. They cooked *pacayas*, the shoots of the palm that grow in the deep ravines of Chimel and El Soch, dipped in egg. At midday, we would do the rounds again with our earthenware pot of *tortillas* to offer to our neighbours. Once again we would eat something at each place we stopped at. . . . Perhaps the nicest thing about Easter was that we knew we would have more than enough bread.[12]

A SIMPLE HOME

The family home was a simple straw hut with wooden struts. Corncobs hung near the door, and the family's animals often grazed nearby. Apple and peach trees grew close to the house, as did a bed of wild passionflowers. There was an almost constant smell of damp earth.

Rigoberta was born in Chimel and lived in the hut until she was 10. She returned again as a teenager, before military units came into the region and drove the people from their homes. Menchú described Chimel as "the place where the first seeds of revolutionary consciousness were sown, the seeds of struggle, of democracy."[13]

CHAPTER 3

The Story of All Poor Guatemalans

Rigoberta Menchú has said that in many ways, her story is the story of all poor Guatemalans. To understand Menchú's life and her mission, it is important to begin with an understanding of her native land and the politics that led to civil war during much of her life.

Guatemala is the most populated country in Central America. It is bordered on the west by Mexico; on the east by Belize, the Caribbean Sea, and Honduras; and on the south by El Salvador and the Pacific Ocean. It is also the largest of the Central American countries; it is slightly smaller than the state of Tennessee.

Long before Europeans conceived of traveling across the oceans, the Mayans built great cities and temples, the ruins of which today offer proof of a highly advanced civilization. Mathematics, philosophy, and astronomy all formed part of this Mayan culture, and in the sixteenth century, the epic work *Popul Vuh* ("Book of Council"), written in Quiché Maya, first appeared. The Mayans by then had begun to disperse, driven by internal conflicts and other unknown reasons. They formed some 30 separate—and often warring—Mayan

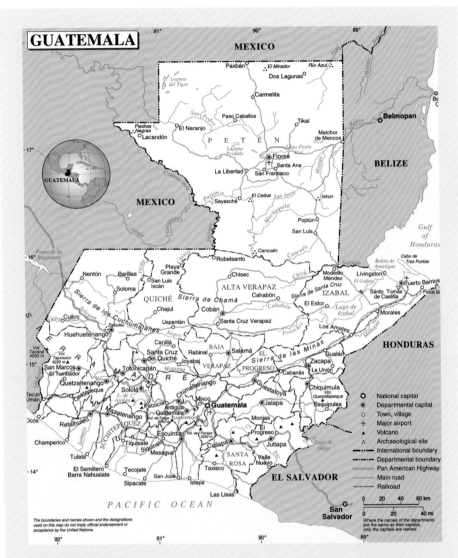

GUATEMALA

The map above shows the country of Guatemala. The Quiché region, where Rigoberta Menchú was born, is located in the central portion of the country.

kingdoms. Some settled in the Yucatán Peninsula of Mexico, others in the *altiplano* ("highlands") of Guatemala. The 21 different present-day Mayan dialects are descended from these different Mayan kingdoms.

At the time that Europeans first arrived in Guatemala, the K'iche' empire was dissolving. At one point, its king, Quicab the Great, had ruled over more than a million subjects. In 1523, the Spanish explorer Hernán Cortés sent one of his captains, Pedro de Alvarado, to explore the region we now know as Guatemala. Alvarado was accompanied by 120 horsemen, 300 foot soldiers, and several hundred Mexican auxiliaries, as well as two priests.[14] They crossed Guatemala from the Pacific to the highlands, eventually encountering a far larger K'iche' army, led by their king, Tecún Umán, grandson of Quicab the Great. The K'iche' far outnumbered the Spaniards, but they were not used to fighting cavalry wearing armor. Their arrows and leather shields were little match for the Spaniards' artillery and steel weapons. King Tecún Umán was killed by Alvarado, and his army soon surrendered.

Next, Alvarado captured and killed the K'iche' nobles. He gradually conquered all of the remaining Mayan tribes, joining with some to defeat their enemies before turning on and seizing them. Those who resisted were massacred. By 1697, all Mayan kingdoms in the highlands had been conquered.

In addition to the violence of the conquest, the arrival of Spaniards in Guatemala brought another threat that killed many more Mayans: European diseases, against which the Mayans had no resistance, quickly spread from the conquerors to the conquered. Hundreds of thousands died from plague, smallpox, yellow fever, influenza, and diphtheria.

The Spanish conquest led to a system of class distinction that still exists in Guatemala today. At the top are the Europeans, called criollos, who were generally the landowners and generals at the beginning. As they settled and produced children with the Mayans, however, these mixed-race offspring, called ladinos, formed a second class. They were considered superior to the Mayans and were given positions as officers and administrators. Those at the bottom of the social order were the indigenous Mayans, referred to as "Indians," who were denied the rights and privileges given to the criollos and ladinos.

These class distinctions persisted for centuries. Rigoberta Menchú would recall her shock when she realized that there were ladinos who were peasants, too. She had always been taught that ladinos looked down upon Indians because of their language, their clothes, and their customs. Menchú did not identify herself as a Mayan; she would in her writing and speeches refer to herself either as Indian or as K'iche'. In her mind, ladinos were the privileged; Indians (or the indigenous peoples) were the oppressed.

COLONIAL RULE

In 1541, the Spanish set up a capital in Antigua, Guatemala. For the next 300 years, the Spanish ruled over Central America. Franciscan, Dominican, and Mercedarian missionaries arrived; they were charged with converting the hundred of thousands of Indians to Catholicism.

The land was divided into huge estates, called haciendas. Royal grants, or titles to these lands, were distributed, and included the right of the owner to claim labor from all Indians living on the estate. The Indians were expected to work without pay and also to provide their master with regular gifts, such as woven goods, produce, or poultry.[15]

Modern Guatemala still bears the scars of this colonial past. The large landowners—about 300 families—control more than 65 percent of the arable land, and large plantations produce coffee, sugarcane, bananas, and cotton. The majority of army officers were ladinos during Rigoberta's childhood and young adulthood, and indigenous peasants continued to be forced to work on plantations in conditions closely resembling slavery.

REBELLION AND EXPLOITATION

Guatemala won independence from Spain in 1821. Later in the nineteenth century, a ladino leader named Rafael Carrera organized a peasant rebellion against the colonial administrators

The photograph above, taken around the beginning of the twentieth century, shows explorers examining a Mayan monument in Guatemala. The Mayan civilization had a long history in what is now Guatemala and other Central American countries.

still in place in Guatemala. In 1840, the rebels assaulted the capital and seized control of the government. For the next 30 years, Carrera or his supporters ruled Guatemala.

In the late 1870s, however, Justo Rufino Barrios came to power. Barrios was a so-called reformer who championed a number of laws that revoked Mayan titles to ancestral lands. In one year, 1884, more than 100,000 acres of Mayan-owned municipal lands passed into private ownership.[16] Huge coffee plantations were formed along the Pacific coast, and Indians who had never traveled from their small plots of land were transported to the coffee plantations and forced into labor.

These laws remained in effect until 1934, when Guatemalan dictator Jorge Ubico passed what he called "vagrancy laws." Any farmer who owned less than two hectares (about five acres) of land was forced to do manual labor for at least 100 days per year. Plantation owners were thus guaranteed the regular arrival of migrant workers at harvest time.

Ubico remained in power for another 10 years, retiring in 1944. His successor was quickly overthrown by an alliance of military officers, students, businessmen, and politicians, who began instituting reforms designed to bring democracy to Guatemala.

This period of social reform and economic modernization came to a sudden halt in 1954, however. The government was violently overthrown in a coup led by Colonel Carlos Castillo Armas, with support from the U.S. Central Intelligence Agency (CIA), landowners, rightwing politicians, and others.[17]

The coup brought a return to domination by the military and the wealthy landowners. The CIA had provided support for the coup based on an American fear of the spread of communism in Central America; Armas's government focused on national security and anticommunism.

The military grew in power and influence in this new regime, spreading out from the cities to more remote villages, focused on keeping order and stamping out any form of protest. Repression became an integral part of this society, along with a growing chasm between those with power and those without. "So final is the repression," one author noted as recently as

Carlos Castillo Armas stands in the doorway of his headquarters
in Esquipulpas, Guatemala, in 1954. Armas, an anticommunist rebel,
led the CIA-backed revolt that overthrew the government and establi-
hed him as leader of Guatemala.

1989, "that the country has no political prisoners—there are just bodies and disappearances."[18] It was into this Guatemala that Rigoberta Menchú was born, a Guatemala controlled by a brutal military dictatorship, where the suffering of the indigenous population was ignored.

CHAPTER 4

Interrupted Childhood

The story Rigoberta Menchú has told of her early life, the story that forms the core of her autobiography *I, Rigoberta Menchú*, has in recent years been marred by controversy. Research and extensive interviews with witnesses and members of her own family have revealed flaws in her story—inaccuracies that raise troubling questions.

Whether the cruelty and oppression Menchú described actually took place is not the subject of the debate. What is questioned is Menchú's accuracy in describing herself as a first-person witness. It is certain that much of what Menchú described actually happened; the question is whether it happened to her.

How can we resolve this dilemma? For the purposes of this book, we will first allow Menchú to present her story in the way it is presented in her books, *I, Rigoberta Menchú* and *Crossing Borders*. We will allow her to speak not only for herself, but also as a witness to horrors experienced by many Guatemalans. In a later chapter, we will review the findings of those who have questioned Menchú's account.

THE PLANTATION

In *Crossing Borders*, Menchú described the demands of her native land: "It takes courage to live here. You really have to want to. You need courage, a lot of patience and much strength."[19]

As a young child, Rigoberta quickly discovered how the racist policies of the government impacted her family. Like many Indians, Rigoberta's family was drafted into seasonal service working on the fincas, the plantations along the Pacific coast.

In *I, Rigoberta Menchú*, Menchú described the horrific trip the family made by truck from their home in the mountains to the plantations on which they would be forced to work. During a journey that could last two days and two nights, 40 people plus their animals (dogs, cats, chickens) were crammed into a stuffy truck covered with a tarpaulin. Each worker brought with him a plate, a cup, and a water bottle. Menchú wrote that she made the journey even as an infant, wrapped in a shawl on her mother's back.[20] The smell would be unbearable, and the tarpaulin prevented those onboard from seeing the countryside through which they were passing.

Menchú recounted in *I, Rigoberta Menchú* how, from the age of about 8 to 10, she worked on a coffee plantation. After that she worked on the cotton plantations further down the coast, where it was very hot.[21] This annual work resulted from the "vagrancy" law, but also from the exploitation of unscrupulous recruiting agents, called *caporales*. The caporales were usually Indians who had left the community, often to serve in the military. They were hired by the landowners to return to their villages and load up a truck with as many people as they could get inside and travel with them to the plantations, where they would be handed over to overseers and put to work.

The Indians, who were brought in by truck, would seldom, if ever, see the plantation owner for whom they worked. Even if they met him, they would not be able to speak with him, as the landowners all spoke Spanish, a language that few Indians understood. They saw only the caporales, who used insults and shouts

Above, workers separate mature coffee beans at a plantation in Guatemala. In *I, Rigoberta Menchú*, Menchú recounted the time she spent
working on coffee plantations such as this when she was a young girl.

to order them to work, and the overseers, who remained on the
plantations.

The workers would receive a small ration of tortilla and
beans. Children too young to work would not be given any food;
it was up to the parents to share their food with their youngest
children. Many families would arrive with 9 or 10 children; few
had enough to eat and everyone was hungry. The workers had to
pay for any additional food over and above their small ration of
tortilla and beans.

Many traps made it impossible for the laborers to earn any
money when their labor was completed for that season. A small
shop on the plantation was stocked with exorbitantly priced
sweets and soft drinks, designed to appeal to hot, tired, and hungry children. Workers would be charged for purchases at the shop,

for food, and for any medicine needed from the pharmacy. If a child accidentally broke the branch of a coffee bush, the parents would be forced to pay for the damage.

Perhaps the greatest trap to the workers was the plantation's *cantina*, owned by the plantation owner. Here, alcohol was served—again, at exorbitantly high prices—to workers who did not realize how high a debt they were accumulating with every drink.

At the end of their labor on the plantation, the workers would go to collect their pay. At that time, however, they would also be presented with the debts they had incurred on the plantation— debts for food, alcohol, and medicine. Often, at the end of a month of grueling work, the laborers would find themselves with no pay.

In *I, Rigoberta Menchú*, Menchú explained her role as a child on the plantation:

> I worked from when I was very small, but I didn't earn anything. I was really helping my mother because she always had to carry a baby, my little brother, on her back as she picked coffee. It made me very sad to see my mother's face covered in sweat as she tried to finish her workload, and I wanted to help her. But my work wasn't paid, it just contributed to my mother's work. I either picked coffee with her or looked after my little brother, so she could work faster.[22]

Menchú wrote of watching her mother work long hours, trying to make enough money to pay for the medicines her children needed. She told of wanting to work so that she could help her mother.[23] In her autobiography, Menchú wrote that she began earning money on the plantation at the age of eight. "I set myself the task of picking 35 pounds of coffee a day. In those days, I was paid 20 *centavos* (about $0.03 U.S.) for that amount. If I picked the 35 pounds, I earned 20 centavos a day, but if I didn't, I had to go on earning those same 20 centavos the next day."[24] Menchú wrote of working late into the evening, picking the coffee bean by bean, gathering up the beans that had fallen from the ground, and picking it from each branch while being careful not to bend or break any of them.

For two years, Menchú wrote, she was paid only 20 centavos a day, even when she picked more coffee. Finally, at the age of 10, when she was picking 70 pounds of coffee a day, she was earning 35 centavos (about $0.05 U.S.).[25]

At times, families would be separated, depending on where labor was needed. Rigoberta's father might be needed on a sugar-cane plantation, cutting and cleaning the sugarcane. Her brother might be sent to pick cotton, whereas Rigoberta and her other brothers and sisters would stay with their mother, picking coffee. They would only be reunited when the work was finished; some-times they were separated for one, two, or three months at a time.

The conditions were awful. The plantations had no toilet facilities, only an open latrine set up in the hills for the approxi-mately 400 workers to use in shifts. There were flies and mos-quitoes everywhere. The laborers were housed in sheds or shacks with open sides; there were no walls, and the roof was only banana leaves or palm leaves. All 400 workers were housed in a single shack. Workers from the same village were seldom housed together; more often they were living beside people who spoke a different dialect and whose customs and habits were completely different. There was no running water in the shed where they were housed; they had to go to the water holes used for irrigating the coffee to get water to drink.

"We had to get up at three in the morning and start work straight away," Menchú recalled in her autobiography.

> It's worst when we're picking cotton because it isn't the weight that counts, it's the quantity. In the early morning it's nice and cool but by midday it's like being in an oven; it's very, very hot. That's why they make us start work so early. We stop work at midday to eat but go on working straightaway afterwards until night-time.[26]

Above, an eight-year-old boy carries sugarcane during a working day in rural Guatemala. Menchú and her siblings had to do similar work as children in order to help their family survive.

A BROTHER'S DEATH

One of the most moving passages in *I, Rigoberta Menchú* involves Menchú's description of the death of her younger brother, Nicolás, when she was eight. According to Menchú, two of her brothers died while the family was working on the plantations.[27] The oldest, Felipe, died before Rigoberta was born, a victim of the pesticides sprayed on the coffee. Felipe breathed in the fumes, and they suffocated him.

Menchú claimed to have witnessed her two-year-old brother's death from malnutrition. According to Menchú, her brother had been ill from the time the family arrived on the plantation, crying constantly as his stomach swelled from malnutrition.[28] "The time came when my mother couldn't spend any more time with him or they'd take her job away from her. . . . My mother kept on working and so did we. He lasted 15 days and then went into his death throes."[29]

Menchú's book depicts a nightmarish scene. Her father was away, working on a different plantation. The family was surrounded by people who spoke a different dialect. They could not communicate with anyone who might help them, and they were afraid that the overseer might throw them off the plantation. According to Menchú, her brother died early in the morning. The overseer told Rigoberta's mother that she could bury him on the plantation, but she would she need to pay a fee to do so. One of the other workers provided the family with a small box to bury him in. "We lost practically a whole day's work over mourning my brother," Menchú wrote:

> We were all so very sad for him. That night the overseer told us: "Leave here tomorrow." "Why?" asked my mother. "Because you missed a day's work. You're to leave at once and you won't get any pay. So tomorrow I don't want to see you round here." It was terrible for my mother, she didn't know what to do. She didn't know how to find my father because he was working somewhere else. When they throw people out of the finca, they don't take them back home as they usually do. Usually when the time comes to go back to the Altiplano, the same contracting agents take us back to our village, so we don't have to worry about how we're getting back, or about any transport, or even where we are. We didn't know our whereabouts, we didn't know where we were or anything. My mother didn't even know the name of the town we were in. But we knew we had to leave so my mother began getting our things together.[30]

The family had worked for 15 days, but they were not paid for those days of labor. They were told that they owed too much to the pharmacy, but Rigoberta's brother had died because the family had not been able to afford any medicine. Rigoberta's mother borrowed enough money to get the family back to their home in the highlands, and sorrowfully they returned to Chimel. Menchú continued:

> My mother was very sad, so was my brother who was with us. My father didn't know his son had died, nor did my other brothers and sisters because they were working on other fincas. Fifteen days later, they all arrived home to be greeted by the news that the little boy had died and that we owed a lot of money. . . . From that moment, I was both angry with life and afraid of it, because I told myself: "This is the life I will lead too; having many children, and having them die." It's not easy for a mother to watch her child die, and have nothing to cure him with or help him live. Those fifteen days working in the *finca* was one of my earliest experiences and I remember it with enormous hatred. That hatred has stayed with me until today.[31]

HARD WORK IN THE HIGHLANDS

When the family was at their home in the altiplano—the highlands—life was still difficult. There was still hard work to be done, but all of the work contributed directly to the family's livelihood. According to Menchú, the family alternated seasons at the plantations with seasons at their home, spending December at the plantation, January and February working the land and sowing the crops in the altiplano, and then returning to the plantation in March for more labor.[32] The seasons were spent in this way, between the plantations and the highlands.

Menchú described her time in the altiplano, noting that she helped her father in the fields from the age of nine.

> I was like a boy, chopping wood with an axe, or with a machete. There was very little water near our village. We had to walk about four kilometers [2.5 miles] to fetch our water, and that added to our work a lot. But we were happy because

Indigenous Mayan women wash their clothes in a lake, above. When Rigoberta Menchú was growing up, Sunday was wash day, and Rigoberta would go with her sister and sister-in-law to wash clothes in the river.

that was the time of year we sowed our bit of maize and it was sometimes enough for us to live on.[33]

Maize, the corn crop, formed the staple of the K'iche' diet. Corn was used to make tortillas, and occasionally beans supplemented the family's meals. There was also chile, bought in the market with the beans the family had grown.

Rigoberta also helped with the household chores. She turned the corn mixture into dough by grinding it with a stone. She built a fire to heat water. The tortillas needed to be made, and maize needed to be toasted and ground to make *pinol*, a cheap alternative to coffee. There was weaving to be done, and younger siblings to be cared for.

At the age of 12, in keeping with K'iche' custom, Rigoberta was given a little pig, a lamb, and two chickens. The animals had to be fed and cared for; she added this to her other responsibilities.

Sunday was wash day, and Rigoberta would go with her sister and sister-in-law to wash clothes in the river. Her parents would go to the market (almost a day's walk), on occasion, to sell their beans or maize and buy the few supplies they needed—soap, salt, and some chile.

At about that time, Rigoberta became more involved in the community and in the Catholic Church. She was chosen to become a catechist, a religious instructor who taught the basics of the Catholic faith to others. The priests would travel from region to region, arriving in Rigoberta's village every three months. Rigoberta would work mainly with the small children, teaching them elements of Catholicism. Menchú described herself as illiterate at the age of 12, and since she couldn't read or write, she had to learn the stories by heart before teaching them to others.[34]

The village organized a Catholic service on Monday afternoons. There would be prayers, hymn singing, and a discussion of village matters. "My community always loved me very much," Menchú recalled, "right from when I was very little. They'd tell me all their sorrows and their joys, because my family had been there for a very long time."[35]

TURNING POINT

When Rigoberta was 14, she was at the finca (the plantation) working with a friend, picking cotton. The cotton fields were sprayed with pesticides, and Rigoberta's friend, Maria, died from the toxic spray.

Those from the village decided not to work for two days, as an expression of grief. Menchú remembered this as a turning point in her life. She thought about how many had died on the finca. She thought about her mother's life—the hardships, the grief, the crippling poverty. "This made me very angry and I asked myself what else could we do in life? I couldn't see any way of avoiding living as everyone else did, and suffering like they did. I was very anxious."[36]

Menchú said in *I, Rigoberta Menchú* that it was at this point that she decided to learn to read.[37] According to her autobiography, she asked her father to talk to the priests, to see if perhaps a scholarship to school could be arranged, but her father refused, saying that if she attended school, she would soon decide to leave the community.[38] More recent research into her life has suggested that, in fact, Rigoberta did attend schools, and that her father was not opposed to an education for his daughter. We will examine these contradictions later in this book.

On their final trip to a finca as a family, Rigoberta's father was approached by one of the landowners, who wanted to take Rigoberta to work for him as a maid. Her father refused, saying, "I couldn't bear my daughter to suffer somewhere far from us. It's better to suffer together."[39]

Rigoberta's elder sister did leave the family to work as a maid. After a few weeks, she returned to the family, disgusted by those she had been forced to wait upon. Menchú, however, knew only that she wanted a life different from the one she had—a life with a future, a life with hope. She decided to travel to the capital to find work as a maid.

CHAPTER 5

In Service

In her autobiography *I, Rigoberta Menchú*, Menchú described working as a maid for a ladino couple and their three children in Guatemala City. She explained that by this time she could understand a little Spanish, but she could not yet speak it.[40] Speaking Spanish was critical, because her employers spoke to her only in Spanish. There was another maid in the household, an indigenous girl, who at first treated Rigoberta with indifference, but eventually befriended her.

Rigoberta was given a small mat in a back room, where the trash was kept. This was her bed. The family's dog was fed meat, rice, and scraps from the meals, but Rigoberta was given only a few beans and some stale tortillas. Her mistress ordered her to buy herself some new clothing, then deducted the cost from her pay.

Rigoberta had to learn how to dust, clean toilets, and iron—tasks she had never done before. In *I, Rigoberta Menchú*, she wrote that while she worked as a maid, she learned Spanish. She spent eight months in that position, until her brother came to tell her that their father, Vicente Menchú, was in prison.

When Rigoberta was 14, she decided that she wanted a life different from the one her family had. She traveled to Guatemala City, the capital of Guatemala, to work as a maid for a ladino couple. Above is a photograph of "El Incienso," a shantytown in the center of Guatemala City.

Rigoberta left her job to visit her father at Santa Cruz prison:

> My father was there with the other prisoners. They were hitting each other, biting each other, and most of them were mad. He was there among all these people. Some of them had fleas. They ate with their hands and were constantly fighting. You could see blood on all their faces.[41]

Vicente Menchú had been imprisoned as a result of the ongoing dispute over the family's land. To win his release, Rigoberta, her family, and the whole community set to work to raise money. Rigoberta and her brothers and sisters returned to the finca to work. Her mother went to work as a maid. After a little more than a year, enough money was raised so that her father could be released.

UNION INVOLVEMENT

According to Menchú, her father had become involved with unions as a result of his battle to secure his land. These unions soon became tangled with the revolutionary movement that was sweeping the region. Vicente's involvement—no matter how marginal—made him a target, and about three months after his release from prison, he was kidnapped, tortured, then left for dead. He did not die, but his wounds were so severe that he had to be hospitalized for nine months.

Shortly after recovering from these injuries, he was again imprisoned briefly. This time, according to Menchú, "they considered him a political prisoner. . . . He was a Communist, a subversive, they said."[42] Vicente Menchú was imprisoned only for 15 days, but during this time, he apparently met up with another political prisoner, who explained why the peasants needed to join together to reclaim their lands. According to Menchú, at this point Vicente decided to join the Comité de Unidad Campesina (CUC)—the Peasants' Unity Committee.

Some have called into question Vicente's involvement with the CUC. What is certain is that, until this time, Vicente's crusade had been a very personal one—an effort to secure the rights to his land. After his imprisonment, however, he became part of a far broader campaign—a campaign that would ultimately attempt the overthrow of the Guatemalan government.

A REVOLUTIONARY BEGINNING

The guerillas who began to rise up in the highlands of Guatemala were inspired by the successful revolutions in Cuba and Nicaragua. They first drafted support from disaffected ladinos, then sought refuge and supplies in the mountains. There, they were able to capitalize on long-existing disputes over land to encourage peasants to join their campaign.

According to Menchú, her father's activities became dangerous enough that, from 1977 on, he went into hiding, leaving the family to avoid endangering them. He would visit the family rarely, and then only at night.

In *I, Rigoberta Menchú*, Menchú recalled this as the beginning of her interest in politics. "I tried to talk to people who could help me sort my ideas out. I wanted to know what the world was like on the other side. I knew the finca, I knew the altiplano. But what I didn't know was about the problems of the other Indians in Guatemala."[43]

She befriended people from other villages in the Uspantán region. She talked with them about their customs, about the food they ate: "It gave me a lot to think about. I have to tell you that I didn't learn my politics at school. I just tried to turn my own experience into something which was common to a whole people."[44]

GROWTH OF THE CUC

The CUC was successful in gaining support from a number of Guatemalan peasants. It emphasized that exploitation, not fate, was responsible for the peasants' suffering. It revealed to the peasants how discrimination and cultural oppression had kept the wealthy in power.

When guerillas began to stage raids on government targets, the army was quickly sent into the highlands to stamp out the guerilla movement. Their methods were brutal and their choice of targets often random. Consequently, many peasants who did not share the revolutionary ideals of the guerilla movement, and had no involvement with the so-called Army of the Poor, were falsely accused, kidnapped, tortured, and murdered.

Although it is certain that there were some peasants who sympathized with the guerilla movement, some may have been guilty of nothing more than hospitality—supplying strangers in their villages with food. Others were falsely denounced by neighbors with a grudge. Still others were simply in the wrong place at the wrong time. The army did not ask questions; anyone suspected of aiding the guerillas—or being a guerilla—was murdered. Entire villages would eventually be destroyed, simply as part of a quest to eliminate the guerilla threat. Many joined the guerilla movement simply for their own protection, after their families and villages had been destroyed.

According to *I, Rigoberta Menchú*, the community at Chimel began to organize for its own protection from the army. Meetings were held, and the community decided that if the soldiers targeted their village, they would respond with force. Menchú wrote that she worked with the children; she taught them Spanish and helped them prepare to defend themselves. She shared her political views.

Menchú also noted in her autobiography that she formed a women's group, her father's prominence in the community giving her an authority she might not otherwise have had. "The moment I learned to identify our enemies was very important to me," she wrote. "For me now the landowner was a big enemy, an evil one. The soldier too was a criminal enemy. And so were all the rich."[45]

Word of violence in nearby communities added to the urgency of the preparations. Then the military arrived in Chimel, Rigoberta's village. Ninety soldiers came, staying in the community meeting house and then at night going into the fields and helping themselves to the crops. When the soldiers finally left, the community decided to prepare for future invasions.

Those living in more remote parts of the village were encouraged to move closer. Huts were built in the center of the village so that the community members could live near one another. Traps that had been used to protect the crops from wild animals were converted to be used against soldiers. Large ditches with invisible nets formed a barrier around the crops and the village.

Because there were no roads, the soldiers would need to travel on foot. They could more easily be trapped on foot than in an army vehicle.

Menchú also wrote of helping to organize escape routes for the villagers. The men needed to leave first—men would be more likely to be seized by the soldiers and tortured for information about guerilla activity, or they would be forced to join the army. Underground paths were dug that led to safe havens far from the village.

Small huts were built at the four corners of the village, and day and night someone was charged with keeping watch at those posts. A signal was arranged, to be spread through the village if an enemy was spotted.

Weapons were gathered. They were simple—machetes, stones, hot water, chile, salt, and lime (the latter two to be thrown into an attacker's eyes).

When the army returned, the signal was spread and the villagers quickly retreated to safety. They sent out scouts, including a pretty girl who chatted with one of the soldiers, distracting him until the scouting party could capture him. They seized his weapons and his uniform, redressing him in peasant clothing. They blindfolded him, then all the mothers of the village talked to the soldier, pleading with him to protect their children. They kept him for several hours and then sent him back to the army, where he was killed for abandoning his post.

The army did not return to the village for a long time. Menchú wrote that she decided to travel to other villages, to teach other communities the defensive techniques that had kept her village safe.

It is important to note that this account of Menchú's life—her time training her village in resistance skills—has also been disputed by reporters and scholars who have retraced her steps. They have suggested that at this period in her life, Menchú was not in the village; she was instead away from home at boarding school. Later, as her father's revolutionary activities brought increased danger to the family, she was smuggled into Mexico.

In her second book, *Crossing Borders*, Menchú did not discuss her revolutionary activity in the village. She discussed instead that of her father, her brother Nicolás, and her two younger sisters. She noted that she left out the details of her life in the CUC to protect the lives of other members of the organization, and that she deleted additional parts that referred to her village.[46] In *Crossing Borders,* she described the purpose of *I, Rigoberta Menchú* as "a historical memory of a people," and noted, "One day I will tell the whole truth."[47]

A FAMILY SEPARATED

According to *I, Rigoberta Menchú*, the last time all of Menchú's family was together was in 1978. Her father had returned briefly to Chimel, and so had she. A fiesta was held in her father's honor, and he spoke words of farewell to his children: "From now on, the people will be your father. The enemy will perhaps take our small lives, but we must try to protect them and defend them to the last. But if there is no other way, have faith and hope in your father the people, because the people will look after you as I do."[48]

In Menchú's autobiography, this is the point when the family committed itself more deeply to revolutionary work.[49] Many of those associated with the CUC or the Army of the Poor—the guerilla movement—left the village and hid in the mountains. Menchú noted that both she and her father left soon after this last gathering.

It was also in 1978 that the campaign of violence began in earnest in the region. In order to stamp out all guerilla activity and frighten any who might be supporting the guerillas, the Guatemalan army began targeting the villages of the highlands. Military camps were set up in many of the villages. Kidnappings, rapes, and torture soon followed. Bodies of those who had been seized would be piled in pits.

Rigoberta's youngest brother, Petrocinio, became a victim of these massacres in 1979. He was 16 years old and living at home with his mother and two younger sisters. He worked in another village, and at some point while traveling between home and work, he was seized and beaten. His captors used torture to force him to reveal the guerillas' hiding place and the location of his family. In *I, Rigoberta Menchú*, Menchú described her brother being tortured for 16 days:

> They cut off his fingernails, they cut off his fingers, they cut off his skin, they burned parts of his skin. Many of the wounds, the first ones, swelled and were infected. He stayed alive. They shaved his head, left just the skin, and they also cut the skin off his head and pulled it down on either side and cut off the fleshy part of his face. My brother suffered tortures on every part of his body, but they took care not to damage the arteries or veins so that he would survive the tortures and not die.[50]

According to *I, Rigoberta Menchú*, Rigoberta and her family (including her parents) received notice that a group of captured guerillas were going to be punished in the public square of the village of Chajul on September 24. They traveled by foot through the mountains, walking nearly all night. They reached Chajul at 8:00 A.M. to find the village surrounded by soldiers. One of the officers gave a speech, announcing that a group of guerillas had been caught and would be punished for being communists and subversives.

Menchú wrote movingly of her mother walking past the tortured prisoners, searching for her son and finding him at last, beaten and barely recognizable:

> All the people were crying, even the children. I was watching the children. They were crying and terrified, clinging to their mothers. We didn't know what to do. During his speech, the captain kept saying his government was democratic and gave us everything. What more could we want? He said that the subversives brought foreign ideas, exotic ideas that would only lead us to torture, and he'd point to the bodies of the men. If

we listened to these exotic slogans, he said, we'd die like them. He said they had all kinds of weapons that we could choose to be killed with. The captain gave a panoramic description of all the power they had, the capacity they had. We, the people, didn't have the capacity to confront them. This was really all being said to strike terror into the people and stop anyone from speaking. My mother wept. She almost risked her own life by going to embrace my brother. My other brothers and my father held her back so she wouldn't endanger herself. My father was incredible; I watched him and he didn't shed a tear, but he was full of rage. And that was a rage we all felt. But all the rest of us began to weep, like everyone else. We couldn't believe it, I couldn't believe that had happened to my little brother. What had he done to deserve that? He was just an innocent child and that had happened to him.[51]

The victims were then set on fire, and the army withdrew. "My mother was half dead with grief," Menchú noted. "She embraced her son, she spoke to him, dead and tortured as he was. She kissed him and everything, though he was burnt. I said to her: 'Come, let's go home.'"[52]

Author David Stoll, in retracing Menchú's steps for his book *Rigoberta Menchú and the Story of All Poor Guatemalans*, found evidence that supported Menchú's story of Petrocinio's torture and murder at Chajul. However, some eyewitnesses have disputed that the victims were set on fire, saying that they were shot. More important, Stoll's interviews revealed that neither Menchú nor her parents were present at her brother's death. According to Stoll,

The important point is not that what really happened differs somewhat from what Rigoberta says happened. The important point is that her story, here and at other critical junctures, is not the eyewitness account that it purports to be. Although she presents her parents, siblings, and self at the scene, Vicente was professing ignorance about the fate of his son shortly before his own death. The Chajules only supposed that the seven victims were from Uspantán because the army said so. In short, no relatives were on hand to identify them, and Rigoberta was not there either.[53]

DEATH AT THE EMBASSY

In late January 1980, peasants from several villages, including Chimel, gathered at the Catholic church in Uspantán. They traveled by bus to Guatemala City and then linked up with a student group from San Carlos University for a protest. Vicente Menchú was with the group. According to some who were part of the original group of peasants, they believed that the purpose of the protest was to demand their rights to land.[54] In *I, Rigoberta Menchú*, Menchú suggested that the trip to the capital was organized "to demand that the army leave El Quiché."[55]

Vicente was clearly the leader of the peasants who participated, but the protest was ultimately directed by the San Carlos students. These students eventually decided that the group would occupy the Spanish embassy to publicize their struggle. The Spanish ambassador was known to be sympathetic to the protestors. Vicente and 6 people from his village, as well as 20 others, arrived at the unguarded Spanish embassy at 11:00 A.M. on January 31, 1980. They were wearing bandanas over their faces as they swept into the embassy, announcing that the 12 people inside, including the Spanish ambassador, were now hostages. They telephoned the media to arrange for a news conference, but before the press could arrive, the embassy was surrounded by riot police and plainclothes detectives.

The ambassador apparently was concerned about an escalation, so he phoned the Guatemalan foreign ministry, the Guatemalan president, and the Spanish foreign ministry to order the police to withdraw. The police cut the phone lines, however.[56] Two Guatemalan dignitaries were in the embassy; they went to

In late January 1980, a group of peasants, including Vicente Menchú, traveled to Guatemala City to stage a protest in cooperation with a group of students. After they occupied the Spanish embassy, it was attacked by the city police, as shown above in this photograph.

the windows with a megaphone, pleading with the police to withdraw, but their pleas were ignored.

About 2:00 P.M., the police began to break into the embassy, smashing doors and windows. The protestors hurried to the second floor, where a metal gate blocked the stairs. They offered to come out in pairs with the hostages and walk to San Carlos University if the police withdrew, but their offer was refused.

The police broke through the metal gate and the protestors retreated to the ambassador's office. They blocked the door with wooden furniture, but the police soon began to break through the door.

Around 3:00 P.M. those gathered outside, including many journalists assembled for the press conference, heard an explosion, then saw smoke and fire. The windows were barred with iron security bars, making escape through the windows impossible. The police blocked the door, preventing firefighters from getting inside the embassy. The screams and cries for help lasted several minutes. In the end, 36 people died at the Spanish embassy, including Rigoberta's father, Vicente Menchú.

THE MYSTERIOUS FIRE

Two people survived the occupation of the Spanish embassy. One was the Spanish ambassador, who had been standing at the door of his office, trying to negotiate with police, when the fire broke out. He burst through the doorway, his hair and clothes on fire.

The other survivor was one of the protestors, found still breathing at the bottom of a pile of corpses near the window. He was rushed to the hospital. The following evening, he was kidnapped from his hospital bed by armed men. His body was discovered at San Carlos University a few days later. He had been shot in the forehead, and a sign left on his body read, "The ambassador of Spain runs the same risk."[57]

The fact that Guatemalan police had invaded the embassy against the ambassador's requests (a violation of international law) sparked tremendous outrage. Spain broke off diplomatic relations with Guatemala. A funeral was held for the protestors three days after the fire, and thousands appeared to mourn them.

The question of who precisely started the fire remains to be answered. Was it the police, or did the protestors themselves set fire to the embassy? In *I, Rigoberta Menchú*, Menchú incorrectly noted that the questions cannot be answered because "no-one from the Spanish embassy siege survived. All of them, every single one died."[58]

In fact, the Spanish ambassador survived. David Stoll interviewed him 15 years later. He confirmed that the protestors had been armed with machetes, three or four revolvers, and Molotov cocktails. Ambassador Cajul was nonetheless sympathetic to the protestors, believing that their intentions were peaceful, and continued to hold the Guatemalan government responsible for the deaths. He did report that during the occupation, one of the protestors spilled gasoline on the floor, intending to light it, and the ambassador himself was forced to stamp out the match tossed onto the fuel with his foot.[59]

Ambassador Cajul added, though, that he was at the door, negotiating with police, when the fire started. It happened behind him; there was an explosion, and then the fire. Cajul also said that he heard shots behind him. "My firm conviction," Cajul told Stoll, "is that the police impeded the departure of all or some of those who found themselves trapped. It appears impossible that no one else could do what I had done [escape through the door], even if I was burned in the process."[60]

DEATH OF MENCHÚ'S MOTHER

The year 1980 brought even more sorrow to Rigoberta Menchú. On April 19, 1980, her mother, Juana Tum Cotojá, was kidnapped. She was living in Chimel at the time, caring for her two youngest daughters and still grieving the loss of her husband.

Guerilla activity had increased in the region, inspired in part by the deaths at the Spanish embassy. Menchú's mother had traveled to the village to get sugar and supplies; she was abducted from the house where she was resting at 11:00 P.M.

Cotojá was questioned by the soldiers who had seized her. When they learned that she was Vicente Menchú's wife, they raped her and tortured her for eight days, demanding to know the whereabouts of her children. She was thrown into a pit and lay there for a long time, dying in agony. In *I, Rigoberta Menchú*, Menchú wrote that her mother's body was eaten by wild animals while the soldiers watched: "They stayed for four months, until they saw that not a bit of my mother was left, not even her bones, and then they went away."[61]

INTO HIDING

It is perhaps not surprising that the brutal deaths of her parents left Menchú shocked and devastated, yet determined to continue their work so that their deaths would not have been in vain. In *I, Rigoberta Menchú*, she wrote of participating in an agricultural workers' strike in February 1980, a strike that lasted 15 days. During the strike, workers sabotaged some of the equipment on the fincas and placed barricades on the roads to block the army's passage. In the end, the workers won a slight wage increase and better food.

Menchú also spoke of participating in a protest on May 1—Labor Day in Guatemala—in 1980. Barricades were erected to block roads in Guatemala City, leaflets were distributed, and strikes and demonstrations were held through the capital city. Factories were notified that bombs had been placed there—a false report to force owners to shut down operations for the day. The protests paralyzed the city for several days.

After these events, Menchú was forced to go into hiding. She had become a target, sought by the army for her participation in the protest. She moved from house to house, often staying with sympathetic nuns or priests. In one convent, she worked as a maid and was forbidden to talk to anyone about her experiences or political views. Finally, she was smuggled out of the country and taken to Mexico.

Her autobiography *I, Rigoberta Menchú* ends here, with Menchú in exile. "I felt a shattered, broken woman," she said, "because I'd never imagined that one day those criminals would force me to abandon my country."[62]

CHAPTER 6

Guatemalan in Exile

R igoberta Menchú fled to Mexico in 1980. She was, at the time, one of many Guatemalans who would flee their country, seeking refuge in the neighboring country. Traveling with a Catholic nun, Menchú ended up in Mexico City, where she attended a conference of Catholic bishops, and shared her life story.

There, she met Monsignor Samuel Ruiz García, who invited her to his home in San Cristobal de las Casas. Ruiz had organized a campaign to help Guatemalan refugees, and Menchú soon became involved in his activities. She spoke at a school for peasant girls run by Mexican nuns. She encouraged them to get an education so they could better help change their society.

Author David Stoll suggested that, contrary to the story told in *I, Rigoberta Menchú*, Menchú did not participate in revolutionary groups before leaving Mexico. His research suggests that her true involvement in the revolutionary movement came later, after she arrived in Mexico and began to work with Monsignor Ruiz and interact with the refugees streaming into Mexico.

Bishop Samuel Ruiz García gives Communion during services in Mexico, above. When Rigoberta Menchú met Ruiz, he was a Monsignor. He invited Menchú to his home when she first arrived in Mexico in exile.

At about this time, in early 1981, three new revolutionary groups had publicly announced their creation in Guatemala. Each was named after someone who had been killed in the fire at the Spanish embassy: the Felipe Antonio García Revolutionary Workers Nuclei, the Trinidad Gómez Hernández Barrio-Dwellers Committee, and the Vicente Menchú Revolutionary Christians. By early 1981, the group named for Menchú's father could claim 4,000 members.[63] These three groups eventually united with the CUC and a student group to form the January 31st Popular Front.

As the daughter of Vicente Menchú, Rigoberta Menchú was welcomed into the movement that bore his name. Within the Revolutionary Christians, Rigoberta's earliest role was as an educator, working with those who joined the organization to help them understand how their country had failed them and what needed to be done to bring change to Guatemala.

Those who did escape from Guatemala into Mexico brought terrible stories of murders and disappearances. Menchú was firmly convinced that she was the only member of her family to survive.

She accompanied Monsignor Ruiz as he traveled from village to village, working with the Mexican poor and the Guatemalan refugees. He encouraged her to take first-aid courses and prepare for work as a health-care provider.

Influences on the Peacemaker

Many people influenced and inspired Rigoberta Menchú throughout her life. First and foremost were her parents. Later, she befriended Guatemalan writer Luís Cardoza y Aragón, and academics Raúl Molina and Rolando Castillo Montalvo. Activist Arturo Taracena helped provide Menchú with the idea of sharing her testimony with Elisabeth Burgos.

Another significant influence on Rigoberta Menchú was Julia Esquivel, a Christian poet from Guatemala, whom Menchú met when both women were living in exile in Mexico. Julia Esquivel de Velasquez was born in San Marcos, Guatemala, in 1930. She studied at the University of San Carlos in Guatemala; the Seminario Biblico Latinoamericano in Costa Rica; and the Ecumenical Institute of Bossey in Switzerland. Trained as a teacher and pastoral social worker, Esquivel quickly became involved in human-rights work during the horrific murders of Guatemala's indigenous population.

Because she spoke out against the oppression, Esquivel was threatened and harassed by police and army personnel. She narrowly escaped several attempted kidnappings, arrests, and assassinations. Finally, she was forced to flee in 1980, in

It was Monsignor Ruiz who one day brought Menchú the joyful news that her two youngest sisters—Anita and Lucía—had been found with a group of Guatemalan refugees who had recently crossed the border. The girls were 10 and 13. After their mother's murder, like many other orphans, they had gone into hiding with the guerillas in the mountains.

In *Crossing Borders*, Menchú noted that shortly after her reunion with her sisters, the three girls were filmed for a television program and also spoke on the radio. For their protection, the girls were given pseudonyms. Menchú, the most fluent in Spanish, did most of the talking, sharing their story.

fear for her life. She found refuge in Mexico, Nicaragua, and Switzerland.

While in exile, Esquivel traveled throughout several countries. She spoke out as a witness to the suffering of Guatemala's indigenous population. She made her way through Europe, the United States, and Canada, and served as an advocate for those who had no voice. Working with churches and rural communities in Guatemala, she has organized global solidarity groups and urged reconciliation and peace.

In her collection of poetry *Threatened With Resurrection* (1994), Esquivel provided a heartrending poetic interpretation of a classic prayer in "The Lord's Prayer from Guatemala," including these lines:

> *Give us this day our daily bread:*
> *The bread of true freedom of the press,*
> *The bread of the freedom to associate and organize,*
> *The bread of living at home and walking the streets without*
> *   being abducted,*
> *The bread of not having to search for a hiding place. . . .*

RETURN TO GUATEMALA

Menchú's sisters were unhappy in Mexico; they wanted to return to Guatemala. Her work with Monsignor Ruiz had inspired in her a desire to work with peasants, to carry on some of the work her father had done:

> I had been working with Monsignor Ruiz when the first refugees started arriving in Chiapas and centres were set up for them. They had walked for days over the mountains. They had no documents, no clothes, nothing. Women had lost small children on the way. They had seen their villages bombed. They had seen massacres. They had seen their houses burned with loved ones inside.[64]

Menchú and her two sisters traveled back to Guatemala, and it was there that Menchú first realized how widely her father's influence had spread. The revolutionary organization that bore his name had helped publicize his actions in organizing and leading the peasant revolutionary movement.

For much of 1981, Menchú worked in the revolutionary movement. She lost many friends to the struggle—some were murdered, others simply disappeared. The group moved often, especially after someone had disappeared. They did not know whether a captured group member might, under torture, reveal their location. There was a constant sense of fear, distrust, and uncertainty.

In this frightening climate, Menchú made a critical mistake. She and her sisters had rented a truck, intending to move items from a compromised location to a new safe house. They did not properly secure one of the boxes they were moving, and as they were traveling to the new location, the box opened and political pamphlets spilled out. The truck driver saw the box open, saw its contents, and turned pale. As they neared a checkpoint patrolled by army soldiers, the women were uncertain whether or not the truck driver would betray them:

We had to pass three patrols of those soldiers who masquerade as police. If we were caught, we would be dead. I remember how terribly frightened we were. Death was so near, I could feel it under my skin. Of course you always say, "I want to give my life for my people. I'd rather be captured dead than alive." But when the time comes, it's as if you say, "No, not now. I'm not ready yet. Maybe later."[65]

Because of their mistake, the location of the new safe house had been compromised. Menchú and her sisters were harshly criticized by the other revolutionaries and told that they could no longer stay with the group—they needed to find their own place to live.

Menchú's sisters decided to return to El Quiché, to rejoin the guerillas with whom they had lived after their mother's murder. Menchú felt guilty about leaving her sisters, but decided to travel to Nicaragua instead. Because she had no visa, she was forced to register as a refugee with the United Nations High Command for Refugees. In this way, she could obtain a UN passport.

In Nicaragua, there was tremendous support for the Guatemalan refugee movement. Menchú quickly came to the attention of the Nicaraguan Committee for Solidarity with Peoples. They organized a press conference at which Menchú was to speak; she stumbled awkwardly through a few prepared lines.

Menchú eventually returned to Mexico to become a member of the Guatemalan Committee for Patriotic Unity. The group focused on providing aid to peasants living in the mountainous jungles of Guatemala. According to Menchú,

They were the survivors of massacres, mainly orphans, widows and old people. Almost all of them were Mayan. They had long used up the few things they had scrabbled together from their houses, and lived in dire conditions. They had no connection with the normal population of Guatemala. They were gradually dying; from malaria, infections, malnutrition and hunger.

On top of all that, they suffered constant harassment from the army. They were chased from place to place, often in torrential rain. Any crops they had managed to plant were destroyed. The army thought they could starve them into surrender. Aerial bombing was also used to try to wipe them out.[66]

Menchú joined with a number of Guatemalan exiles—including journalists, political leaders, writers, and professors. Many of them were ladinos. They all shared a desire to support those left behind in Guatemala.

I, RIGOBERTA MENCHÚ

One of the group's goals was to raise international awareness of the suffering in Guatemala and international support for the revolutionary movement. In January 1982, Menchú formed part of a group that went to Europe as a public symbol of the January 31st Popular Front.

As one of the younger and less experienced spokespeople on the tour, Menchú wrote in *Crossing Borders,* she spent much of the tour listening to others in the group discuss the situation in Guatemala.[67] It was one of the other members of the group, Arturo Taracena, who introduced her to Elisabeth Burgos in Paris, then encouraged the two to collaborate on the story that would become *I, Rigoberta Menchú.*

Elisabeth Burgos had long been a supporter of the Guatemalan refugees. Her husband was a respected philosopher and author, and she, too, was a political refugee—from Venezuela. She had joined the Communist Party in Venezuela, was arrested, and was forced into exile. She met her husband while he was on a journalistic tour. After working to support various revolutionary movements in Latin America, the couple moved to France. There, Burgos had organized solidarity movements in support of Guatemala.

Elisabeth Burgos was working on her doctoral dissertation when she was asked to interview a young Mayan refugee who had just arrived in Paris. Menchú arrived at her interviewer's home one evening in January 1982, dressed in her traditional Mayan clothing, which was ill suited to the cold temperatures. She was not wearing a coat or stockings, and her arms were bare. "The first thing that struck me about her was her open, almost child-like smile," Burgos later wrote. She continued:

> Her face was round and moon-shaped. Her expression was as guileless as that of a child and a smile hovered permanently on her lips. She looked astonishingly young. I later discovered that her youthful air soon faded when she had to talk about the dramatic events that had overtaken her family. When she talked about that, you could see the suffering in her eyes.[68]

For a week, Menchú stayed with her interviewer, telling her story. They began the recordings at 9:00 A.M., broke for lunch at about 1:00 P.M., then continued until 6:00 P.M., occasionally doing additional work in the evening. Burgos had provided an initial outline, suggesting that they should develop Menchú's story by talking first about her childhood, her adolescence, her family, and then her involvement in the revolutionary movement. Menchú soon took over the interview, however; she provided information about K'iche' customs and practices, talked about birth and death, and digressed to add insights about her family, her experiences, and those of her people. Burgos had nearly 18 ½ hours of tapes by the time the interviews were completed.

Elisabeth Burgos then turned the tapes into a manuscript. In the process, she rearranged some of the material to preserve a closer chronological order, divided the material into chapters, and omitted her own questions, turning the dialogue into a monologue. She soon realized that this material might provide an interesting book.

Burgos sent the edited manuscript to Menchú's organization for a security check. The manuscript was returned with some suggested omissions and, in September 1982, it was sent to a publishing house. The book was published in 1983 in Spanish, and in 1984 in French and English.

The book propelled Menchú to international fame. There were certain inaccuracies and inconsistencies in the text, however, that eventually would mar Menchú's receipt of the Nobel Peace Prize. These included questions about Menchú's education, her participation in the resistance movement in Guatemala, her work on the plantations, and her accounts of the deaths of two of her brothers. It is important to note that in her subsequent memoir, *Crossing Borders*, Menchú distanced herself from *I, Rigoberta Menchú*. She noted:

> When I wrote that book, I simply did not know the commercial rules. I was just happy to be alive to tell my story. I had no idea about an author's copyright. . . . I censured several parts that might have been dangerous for people. I took out bits that referred to my village, details about my brothers and sisters, and names of people. That is why the book lacks a more specific identity and I feel it will be my duty to provide this before I die. That is what I still hope to do.[69]

She also noted that the story needed to be retold and finished. "One day I will tell the whole truth," she explained.[70]

SPEAKING OUT

After her tour through Europe, in May 1982, Menchú traveled to the United States. She spoke before small groups, at the invitation of those familiar with the situation in Guatemala—missionary groups and a few small political action groups. She led some workshops for solidarity committees and also lobbied the U.S. Congress and State Department.

In Guatemala, the repression of opposition groups intensified. Many of the groups collapsed because of decreasing membership, infighting, and lack of cooperation among the revolutionary organizations. There was fear on the part of leaders to be too publicly identified as advocating the overthrow of the Guatemalan government. The Popular Front disappeared, as did the Vicente Menchú Revolutionary Christians.

One of the few groups to survive was the Peasants' Unity Committee (CUC). This group survived only outside Guatemala, and Menchú soon became its most well known leader. Her story was always well received; she was a dynamic speaker who had developed a reputation for being able to connect with foreign audiences. As Vicente Menchú's daughter, she could speak in his name, and in the name of all those who were martyred in the revolutionary struggle. She provided a connection to peasants, to those who lived in exile, and to many different, alienated groups.

Menchú noted in *Crossing Borders* that she needed the permission of the CUC leaders to travel anywhere.[71] She was invited by the International Council of Indian Treaties to travel to the United Nations, in Geneva, to lobby for the rights of the Guatemalan Indians, and was given permission by the CUC to go. She received a ticket and the arrangements were made, but when she arrived in Geneva, no one was waiting for her. She spoke no French and couldn't find anyone who understood her Spanish. Finally, she decided to travel to the Nicaraguan embassy, as the Nicaraguans had helped the CUC on many occasions.

The Nicaraguan ambassador met with Menchú and invited her to stay in his home. She gradually began to meet some of the officials at the United Nations. She was one of five or six indigenous people at the UN lobbying for rights. Menchú described the situation:

> We looked like oddballs and we were treated as such. Some officials were offhand and rather suspicious, as if we were

making things up. I think they were embarrassed for us. Others were curious to find out what we had come to the UN for. Nonindigenous friends fighting for indigenous rights were few and far between in those days. For many people, we were insignificant, though for others we were important. People with similar causes and similar sensitivities welcomed us into their homes and gave us the best of what they had to offer.[72]

Menchú began lobbying, telling anyone who would listen about the situation in Guatemala. She was invited to speak at one of the UN sessions. Just as she began, however, the ambassador from Guatemala called for a point of order, which was seconded by delegates from the United States and Morocco. Menchú was forced to yield the floor, and such a commotion followed that the session had to be suspended. The Guatemalan delegation apparently requested that the group that had invited Menchú to speak—the International Council of Indian Treaties—should be removed. This would expel from the United Nations representatives not only from Guatemala, but also from the Navajos, Hopis, Lakotas, and other Native American groups. Finally, Menchú was invited back to the floor and she resumed as if there had been no interruption, saying, "Mr. President, in my country they speak 22 different languages . . . "[73]

Gradually, Menchú was joined by other Guatemalans in the formation of the Unitary Representation of the Guatemalan Opposition (RUOG). The group lobbied the UN and human rights organizations. Menchú became more comfortable speaking in public and less nervous when confronting high-ranking UN delegates. Menchú returned to Mexico City, but continued to travel to the UN to lobby for Guatemalan rights.

The RUOG had an unusual status. It was not an official representative of the opposition movement in Guatemala. It was not a political party. It had no official status at the UN. But Menchú and the others would haunt the corridors of the United Nations, begging a few minutes with this or that delegate to explain their position or to win the right to address a group. She said of the experience:

> On countless occasions, they had to throw me out of the main conference hall. The police would come and tell me, "Madam, this is a government area, you can't come in." I would pretend that I didn't understand English, but they would throw me out anyway. Then I would go back in again. For 12 years I steam-rolled—literally steam-rolled—down the U.N. corridors, battering down all its doors.[74]

Menchú's focus was on publicizing the situation of Guatemala to a group for whom, she knew, Guatemala was simply one small speck in the vast "Third World." Her focus was on publicizing the Guatemalan Indians' rights to life, freedom of organization, and freedom of expression, and how those rights had been denied. The group lobbied to have the UN pass a resolution critical of human rights in Guatemala, an effort that was ultimately successful.

Menchú understood the human-rights campaign as part of a larger struggle, and she followed closely the lobbying of groups from Nicaragua, Cuba, Chile, and El Salvador. "If everybody had the chance to discover the UN the way that I have, we could probably change a lot of things with the laws already in existence," Menchú wrote in *Crossing Borders*. "I managed to learn all this without having any diplomas or university degrees. I have never studied international law and I never will. I simply learned by following UN diplomats and bureaucrats around."[75]

CHAPTER 7

Guatemala in Crisis

While Rigoberta Menchú was lobbying the United Nations, her country was enduring additional horrors. The military government in power had targeted the rural areas of Guatemala; officials decided that by eliminating entire villages, the source of support for the guerillas would also be eliminated.

The early 1980s marked a particularly horrifying chapter in Guatemalan history. Death squads, formed by the army to combat the guerillas, carried out massacres throughout the country. Many of the victims were Indians. To understand Menchú's efforts, which resulted ultimately in her receiving the Nobel Prize, it is important to understand the changes her country was undergoing both before and after her time in exile.

Guatemala had been under military rule for many decades. Elections would be held every four years, but in these elections, the military would preselect its candidate and declare him the winner when the election was over. Violent attacks against the guerillas—and indigenous villages—marked the rule of General Fernando Romeo Lucas García, elected president in 1978. He ruled for several years;

Efraín Ríos Montt is shown here in 2003. On March 23, 1982, retired general Ríos Montt launched a military coup in Guatemala. Under Ríos Montt, the government suspended the constitution, shut down the legislature, and began a campaign to root out political dissidents.

his handpicked successor was installed by the military in March 1982. By the early 1980s, however, divisions within the military had arisen. Some questioned the methods of dealing with the guerillas; others disagreed with the choice of presidential candidate.

On March 23, 1982, a group of military officers, led by the retired general Efraín Ríos Montt, launched a military coup. They marched on the National Palace and forced General Angel Aníbal Guevara to step down, only two weeks after he was installed as president. By June, Ríos Montt had himself installed as president and ruled essentially as a dictator. He made an offer of amnesty to the guerillas, which they rejected. Ríos Montt then launched a brutal antiguerilla campaign that targeted all of the Indians and peasants suspected of giving aid or support to the guerillas.

The key to this campaign was the belief of the Ríos Montt government that all Indians were subversives—that they all supported the guerilla actions against the government. In order to effectively wipe out the guerillas, the government believed, it must wipe out their support amongst the Indians. The genocide that resulted was clearly planned, with the understanding that the possible murder of nearly 150,000 civilians might be necessary to "establish social peace."[76]

In order to wipe out the supposed guerilla support network, the government targeted numerous Indian villages in the highlands. These were burned, many of the villagers were murdered, and the survivors were forced to relocate. More than 440 villages were entirely destroyed; 100,000–150,000 civilians were murdered and one million were left homeless.[77] In addition, wide stretches of the highlands were destroyed in a so-called scorched earth campaign, the forests burned to ensure that the guerillas had no area in which to hide during.

Ríos Montt himself was the victim of a coup in August 1983 and was replaced by his minister of defense, General Oscar Humberto Mejía Víctores. With this coup, formal military rule was reinstated. Steps were taken, though, to move the country toward civilian rule, with the idea that this would help contribute to greater internal security and development for Guatemala. A new constitution was approved in 1984. Menchú actually heard portions of it read by the Guatemalan representatives to the UN. She was inspired to even greater efforts on behalf of Guatemalan Indians when she heard the rights the constitution claimed to guarantee for Guatemalan citizens. In late 1985, elections were held once again. This time, the military did not force its candidate into the presidency, and Vinicio Cerezo began his leadership in January 1986.

The Guatemalan political scene posed an interesting situation: It was a fragile democracy that existed not because of popular demand but because the military had determined that democracy made sense—at least for the time being. The elections, the civilian president, were gifts of the military—gifts that could be retracted.[78] It was a presidency, and a democracy, that depended on the military for its existence.

A THREATENED POPULATION

Although the scorched earth campaign had come to an end, the indigenous population still faced constant threats. Between 1983 and 1985, the military put into place what were called civilian self-defense patrols. Essentially, villagers were forced to participate in efforts to identify and eliminate guerilla activity. Anyone who refused to participate was fined and labeled a subversive.

Next, because so many of the villages had been destroyed, the indigenous population was forcibly moved to in rural resettlement camps controlled by the army. The forests, villages, and farms had been burned, depriving the Indians of their sources of food, shelter, and firewood. In the moved to camps, people were suddenly dependent on the army for food, shelter, and work.

Under Cerezo, efforts were made to invite many of the refugees who had fled Guatemala to return. At the time, there were 150,000–200,000 Guatemalan refugees in Mexico alone.[79] Oversight of returning refugees was left to the army, however, and most of its members considered the refugees subversives. An offer of amnesty was made to the refugees, but if the refugees accepted an offer of amnesty, they would be admitting that they had been

In the 1980s, many people were killed during the violence that wreaked havoc on unstable Guatemala. Many such atrocities were not officially recognized as having occurred until the 2000s. Above, indigenous women take part in the 2006 burial of the remains of 19 people murdered in the early 1980s.

connected to the guerillas. Most refused to return without greater guarantees of their safety, including a promise that they could return to their own villages (rather than to the resettlement camps). As a result, by 1990 only 13 percent of the refugees had returned to Guatemala.[80]

Despite the political efforts and the public face of a government that vowed to distance itself from the era of death squads, in reality, there were still two Guatemalas: one for the wealthy, the ladinos and the landowners, and another for the Indians. The Cerezo government (which lasted from 1986 to 1991) desperately wanted to convey an ideal of unity and peace, in part to receive desperately needed economic aid from an international community that was condemning Guatemala's human rights violations. While the Guatemalan government was trying to portray itself as entering a new chapter in its history, however, a young Mayan woman was gaining international attention for exposing all that had come before.

MENCHÚ RETURNS

In April 1988, Rigoberta Menchú decided to return to Guatemala. She was part of a delegation attempting to arrange peace talks and traveled openly to her country for the first time since her flight eight years earlier.

At the airport, though, she was identified as a participant in the CUC, which meant that she needed to apply for amnesty before being allowed back into the country. She and a companion were driven to prison.

Menchú was not the same peasant girl who had left her country eight years before, however. She had traveled the world and made many influential friends. They quickly mobilized to gain her release. Menchú was arrested at noon; by that afternoon protestors filled the streets of Guatemala City. Many officials—including President François Mitterrand of France—phoned the Guatemalan president to express their displeasure and demand Menchú's immediate release.

That evening, a judge held a hearing and announced that Menchú would be released if she accepted the offer of amnesty. She refused and explained why in *Crossing Borders*:

> The amnesty was introduced specifically for criminals, for paramilitary killers. Its purpose was to allow soldiers involved in the repression and in successive military coups to go unpunished. No less than twelve amnesty laws were passed in ten years, and they all favoured the military. It was another plank in the counterinsurgency plan. . . . This was the same "amnesty" that they offered to us. So we said: "We aren't generals who stage coups, we aren't ex-guerrillas, we haven't come to wage psychological warfare, we aren't murderers, we aren't criminals. We refuse to accept an amnesty."[81]

Menchú's belief was that, if she accepted this amnesty clause, she would admit to having committed a crime and accept an offer of pardon. Because she was firmly convinced that she had done nothing wrong, she refused the judge's order.

Finally, the judge agreed to simply release them, although publicly announcing that he had applied the amnesty law. Menchú felt no sense of relief. Instead, the danger to her and those traveling with her seemed clearer. While they were in custody, anything that happened to them was clearly the work of the government. Once they had been set free, there was an additional risk of reprisal. By her own account, she slept very little during the seven days she spent in Guatemala.

Menchú returned to Guatemala again in February 1989 to participate in a conference sponsored by the Catholic Church. She spoke on behalf of the revolutionary movement, one of the few delegates who dared to do so. She received constant death threats, some sent in the form of invitations to her funeral.

Menchú returned to Guatemala again in 1991, this time to organize a demonstration. Each time, her visits were marked by threats and uncertainty. She could no longer feel at home in the country that had once been her own.

CHAPTER 8

Nobel Prize

The campaign to award the Nobel Peace Prize to Rigoberta Menchú began at a time when Menchú was becoming a well-known international figure but was still little known in her native land. Few Guatemalan Indians could have identified the woman who was bringing their cause to the attention of the world.

The first effort to award the Nobel Prize to Rigoberta Menchú began in Italy in 1989. Shortly after her visit to Guatemala to attend the conference sponsored by the Catholic Church, she traveled to Italy to speak to the Socialist Party. She narrowly escaped a car bomb when leaving Guatemala, and the Italian press published several articles suggesting that Menchú was a logical choice for the Nobel Prize.

The first official nomination came from another winner of the Nobel Peace Prize, Argentinean human-rights leader Adolfo Pérez Esquivel. There is a waiting list for the prize—each year more than 100 candidates are nominated—and some, like Rigoberta Menchú, are nominated more than once. During the years that Menchú was nominated, winners included the Dalai Lama of

Tibet, Soviet leader Mikhail Gorbachev, and Burmese activist Aung San Suu Kyi. Then, yet another Nobel Peace Prize winner joined the call for Menchú's nomination—Bishop Desmond Tutu of South Africa.

At the time, Menchú's focus was undergoing a subtle shift—a result of the changing political climate in Guatemala and of her own interaction with other indigenous leaders lobbying at the UN. Menchú had not previously identified herself as Mayan, but gradually she began to understand herself as part of a Mayan culture, an indigenous people of whose culture and rights her K'iche' customs formed only a portion. The movement for Mayan rights identified Menchú as one of their own, however, and slowly her focus shifted from the revolutionary to the determination to achieve human rights and respect for the indigenous population of Guatemala.

QUINCENTENARY CONFERENCE

It was at the Quincentary ("500 Years") Conference in October 1991 that Menchú truly emerged as a national leader, one identified and recognized by her fellow Guatemalans. Menchú had returned to Quezaltenango, Guatemala's second largest city, to participate in the Second Continental Conference on Five Hundred Years of Indigenous and Popular Resistance. The ceremony marked the 500th anniversary of Christopher Columbus's landing in the Americas, a time many indigenous people point to as the beginning of the oppression of Native Americans. The meeting invited an international audience to celebrate and support the indigenous people of Guatemala and of all the Americas.

Menchú was the star of the meeting, easily identified by the international audience and quickly recognized by the Guatemalans, as well. David Stoll quoted one North American attendee at the conference as saying, "When she showed up at the conference, people screamed out her name. She's a lot bigger than the government would like to admit. Someone was talking about running her for president; lots of Indians would vote for her."[82]

There was, of course, criticism of how much focus was placed on Menchú during the conference. It was becoming clear, however, that Menchú was a possible nominee for the Nobel Prize, and the attention she was receiving—and the attention it brought to the plight of Guatemala's indigenous population—was understood as ultimately leading to international pressure that could provoke change within the Guatemalan government.

The Nobel Prize is chosen by a committee meeting in Norway. Previous laureates (winners of the prize) often speak out in support of a particular candidate, as they did in the case of Rigoberta Menchú. Tradition dictates, however, that the potential nominee should not openly campaign for the honor.

Menchú certainly understood how receipt of the Nobel Prize would help publicize the Guatemalan army's abysmal human-rights record.[83] It would also help encourage Guatemala's indigenous population to organize, to break their silence, and to speak out about their own experiences. It would lend international support to the human-rights campaign in Guatemala.

The international attention also gave a certain amount of safety to Menchú as she increased her travels through Guatemala. As a possible nominee for the Nobel Peace Prize, Menchú could not be threatened—anything that happened to her would draw tremendous international attention and outrage. While she toured much of Guatemala, she avoided one place—the place where she was born.

She confessed in *Crossing Borders* that she was afraid to return to Chimel: "There had been so much violence, so much death, and so much disintegration within the armed struggle itself. No one ever knew who killed whom, or what had happened where. It is a place which holds many mysteries, secret graves, people eaten by animals."[84]

As the rumors of a possible Nobel Prize increased, Menchú remained focused on her work with the CUC. There was recognition among many of its members (including Menchú) that the organization had lost some of its drive since the late 1970s and early 1980s. The members had been scattered; many had been killed or driven into exile. It was harder and harder to find people willing to stand up and speak out against the forces in power in Guatemala.

In 1992, while Menchú was traveling in Guatemala, she met Angel Canil Grave, who was also working for the CUC in a campaign to win land for Guatemala's indigenous population. Menchú

Critics of the Peacemaker

It is perhaps a mistake to label anthropologist David Stoll as a "critic" of Rigoberta Menchú. Stoll is not critical of Menchú's work as a human-rights activist or her position on the atrocities committed against the indigenous people of Guatemala. Rather, Stoll, in his book *Rigoberta Menchú and the Story of All Poor Guatemalans* (published in 1999), identified and corrected the inaccuracies in Menchú's testimony, particularly as published in her life story *I, Rigoberta Menchú*.

Stoll is a professor of anthropology at Middlebury College in Vermont. Before enrolling in Stanford University as a doctoral candidate, he spent 10 years writing about and studying the work of Protestant missionaries in Latin America. While at Stanford, Stoll focused his dissertation work on Guatemala and how its people coped with extensive periods of violence. Stoll traveled to Guatemala in 1989, while the civil war still raged. During this trip he learned, almost in passing, that Menchú's account of her brother Petrocinio's murder contrasted with the memories of the villagers there with whom Stoll spoke. Stoll earned his Ph.D. in 1992, and he continued his research on Guatemala.

Stoll focused on the peace process and the continuing violence in the region, specifically in the Quiché department. His work has led him into controversy, not only for his research on Rigoberta Menchú, but also because he questioned assumptions made by the human-rights movement about the situation in Guatemala.

Stoll's *Rigoberta Menchú and the Story of All Poor Guatemalans* was the result of 10 years of research and hundreds of interviews with members of Menchú's family, witnesses to the scenes she describes in her book, local officials, and villagers.

had vowed many years earlier never to marry and instead to dedicate herself to her work, but Angel changed her mind. She said in an interview several years after their first meeting:

> When I met him, I really didn't think that it was going to be a longstanding relationship. How could it, when I was always

As Stoll himself noted, he never questioned the decision to award Menchú the Nobel Prize—in fact, he felt that the award was "a good idea"—but he still felt that the veracity of her story should be examined and examined carefully. Stoll believed that a careful examination of the truth in Menchú's life story revealed much about how accounts of the violence in Guatemala evolved to meet the needs of the revolutionary movement and its supporters, and that it could challenge any romantic or idealized images about guerrilla warfare and indigenous people.

Stoll's version of the story has inspired its own critics. Rigoberta Menchú has refused to respond to Stoll directly but has suggested that such criticism of *I, Rigoberta Menchú* is racist. Others, including members of the academic community who include *I, Rigoberta Menchú* as part of their course reading, have suggested that the book never claimed to be a completely factual account of events, and that the type of rigorous examination to which it was subjected by Stoll is inappropriate for a work of "collective memory." They believe that thousands of Guatemalans were murdered during the civil war, and whether or not Menchú was an eyewitness is less important than the light her testimony sheds on a little-known global crisis.

Still others have questioned whether or not the villagers to whom Stoll spoke would have been willing to provide a truthful account of events to a stranger, an American academic. Either way, the debate inspired by Stoll's research is an interesting one: How significant is it if certain portions of *I, Rigoberta Menchú* are not truthful? Can Menchú serve as the embodiment of her people's struggle, even if her life experiences were quite different from theirs?

going from one place to another, almost like a vagabond? My husband's family, in particular, helped me a great deal in stabilizing my life. It only happened because my future in-laws were really very persistent and just insisted—all the time—that we get married, even if it was only a civil wedding. They were worried about what the family, what the society, what the community, what everybody else would think if we weren't married. For me, it didn't have any particular importance."[85]

The couple eventually married, in 1995.

THE CHOICE

The Nobel Peace Prize is granted each year to the person who has done the most to work "for the peace and brotherhood of men."

The choice of the award has often generated controversy. The recipients have had wide-ranging backgrounds and philosophies. They have included human-rights activists, conflict mediators, and those working in the field of arms control.

For the 1992 Nobel Peace Prize, 113 prominent men and women were nominated. Among them were former UN Secretary-General Javier Pérez de Cuellar, Václav Havel of Czechoslovakia, and Nelson Mandela of South Africa. It was a noteworthy and distinguished group. Author David Stoll suggested that the international focus on the Quincentenary—the 500th anniversary of 500 years of struggle for indigenous rights, and also the 500th anniversary of Columbus's landing in America—may have been a factor in the choice of a Native American as the laureate.[86]

Rigoberta Menchú was certainly not an easy choice. There was some concern over portions of her autobiography *I, Rigoberta Menchú* that clearly advocated using violence to resist oppression. In addition, it seemed clear that for at least some of her life, Menchú was a member of, and supported, the guerilla movement in Guatemala.

The choice of Menchú was supported by many leading Central American activists, however. They understood and applauded Menchú's efforts to shed light on the human rights violations in Guatemala. Granting the award to Menchú could also signal the Nobel Committee's desire to see the civil war in Guatemala ended once and for all.

Few people are qualified to nominate a candidate for the Nobel Peace Prize. These include members of national assemblies and governments of states; members of international courts; university rectors; professors of social sciences, history, philosophy, law, and theology; directors of peace research institutes and foreign policy institutes; previous recipients of the Nobel Peace Prize; board members of organizations that have received the Nobel Peace Prize; active and former members of the Norwegian Nobel Committee; and former advisors appointed by the Norwegian Nobel Institute.

In September of the previous year, nomination forms are sent to all of those deemed eligible to nominate a candidate. Nominations must be postmarked by February 1, after which the Nobel Committee looks through the letters of nomination. Between March and May, a short list is assembled as the committee evaluates the candidates. In the period from June to August, the short list is evaluated by permanent advisers as well as advisers chosen for their knowledge of a particular candidate. The prize winner is selected in October: The committee members vote, and whomever receives a majority of the votes is chosen the winner. The vote is final; there are no appeals. The winner of the Nobel Peace Prize is announced on the same day the vote is taken. The formal presentation ceremony takes place in Oslo, Norway, on December 10.

THE ANNOUNCEMENT

As we read at the beginning of this book, Menchú was in Guatemala when she learned that she had been chosen as the recipient of the Nobel Peace Prize for 1992. The announcement from the Nobel Committee read:

> The Norwegian Nobel Committee has decided to award the Nobel Peace Prize for 1992 to Rigoberta Menchú from Guatemala, in recognition of her work for social justice and ethno-cultural reconciliation based on respect for the rights of indigenous peoples. Like many other countries in South and Central America, Guatemala has experienced great tension between the descendants of European immigrants and the native Indian population. In the 1970s and 1980s, that tension came to a head in the large-scale repression of Indian peoples. Menchu has come to play an increasingly prominent part as an advocate of native rights.
>
> Rigoberta Menchú grew up in poverty, in a family which has undergone the most brutal suppression and persecution. In her social and political work, she has always borne in mind that the long-term objective of the struggle is peace.
>
> Today, Rigoberta Menchú stands out as a vivid symbol of peace and reconciliation across ethnic, cultural and social dividing lines, in her own country, on the American continent, and in the world.[87]

Little rejoicing came from the administration of Guatemalan president Jorge Serrano Elías at the news that his countrywoman had been awarded the Nobel Prize for Peace. The president eventually issued a short message of congratulations. An army spokesperson noted that Menchú's ties to Guatemala's enemies should have disqualified her from the prize.[88]

Other world leaders were more open in their congratulations, and invitations came to Menchú from the leaders of Mexico, France, Italy, and Spain. She was invited to formal ceremonies at the United Nations and the Vatican, where she met with Pope John Paul II.

Above, Rigoberta Menchú displays her Nobel Peace Prize after receiving the diploma and gold medal from Francis Sejersted (left), chairman of the Nobel Committee. Menchú said that she considered the prize "not as a reward to me personally, but rather as one of the greatest conquests in the struggle for peace. . . ."

In *Crossing Borders*, Menchú described the outpouring of goodwill that came from many people within Guatemala:

There are moments when we should celebrate our nation, our country, and our life, and celebrate it together, especially if we can celebrate something that, in my lifetime, has been no more than an illusion. Peace, to live in peace, no more war. It strengthened my belief in a multi-ethnic, multi-lingual, pluri-cultural society, where indigenous people and *ladinos* can celebrate the nation's triumphs together.[89]

On December 10, 1992, 33-year-old Rigoberta Menchú Tum was in Oslo for the formal ceremony awarding her the Nobel Peace Prize. The award was accompanied by a medal and a cash prize of $1.2 million. Francis Sejersted, chairperson of the Norwegian Nobel Committee, gave the presentation speech. He noted:

> The goal of Rigoberta Menchú Tum's work, as she has said on many occasions, is reconciliation and peace. She knows, better than most, that the foundations for future reconciliation are laid in the manner in which one conducts one's struggle. Even in the most brutal situations, one must retain one's faith that there is a minimum of human feelings in all of us. Rigoberta Menchú Tum preserved that faith.[90]

Menchú's acceptance speech, delivered in Spanish, began with her acknowledgment that the prize was being awarded not to her personally, but "as one of the greatest conquests in the struggle for peace, for human rights, and for the rights of the indigenous people, who, for 500 years, have been split, fragmented, as well as the victims of genocides, repression and discrimination."[91]

She spoke movingly of the struggles of all indigenous people, then turned her attention to the situation in Guatemala:

> The case of the displaced and of refugees in Guatemala is heartbreaking; some of them are condemned to live in exile in other countries, but the great majority live in exile in their own country. They are forced to wander from place to place, to live in ravines and inhospitable places, some not recognized as Guatemalan citizens, but all of them are condemned to poverty and hunger. There cannot be a true democracy as long as this problem is not satisfactorily solved and these people are reinstated on their lands and in their villages.[92]

In her speech, Menchú noted that she would keep her Nobel Prize medal in Mexico City until "peaceful and safe conditions" were established in Guatemala. She also noted that the strongest objections to her receipt of the award had come from her own country, from her own people, where racism and prejudice inspired criticism of an indigenous person winning such a prize. She concluded, however, with a suggestion of hope for the future:

> The peoples of Guatemala will mobilize and will be aware of their strength in building up a worthy future. They are preparing themselves to sow the future, to free themselves from atavisms, to rediscover their heritage. To build a country with a genuine national identity. To start a new life.[93]

CHAPTER 9

Menchú's Legacy

I n *Crossing Borders*, Menchú noted that journalists and admirers often ask her whether her life was changed by the Nobel Peace Prize. She replied:

> On one occasion, I said, "Of course it has changed my life, it has opened a great door and I have been lucky enough to pass through it." It really did change my life, yet it was never going to change it that much. Quite simply, I have always had the same face, the face of a poor indigenous woman, and there is no way in which I can change that. The Nobel Prize is for life, but so too are my beliefs and my origins.[94]

To illustrate how Menchú's battles have changed little since her receipt of the Nobel Prize, Menchú related the story of an incident that took place in Minneapolis after she had become the Nobel laureate. She had traveled to the United States to attend a Nobel Peace Institute conference, but at the airport she was detained by an overly zealous customs official. The woman questioned Menchú, then handed her over to another immigration official for additional questioning. When Menchú refused to respond to certain questions, the official threatened to withdraw her visa.

Airline officials attempted to intervene, but the immigration supervisor was called in. When Menchú refused to answer questions without an attorney present, she was told that she had no right to see an attorney.[95] Finally, the questioning came to an end, after an hour and a half. Menchú recounted,

> When I finally got away, I though how wonderful it was to receive the Nobel Prize. It meant respect, red carpets, tributes, all sorts of things. Then, as we left the airport, I thought to myself, "The Nobel Prize may have changed my life, but this has been a test, my first since I received the Prize. I'm glad I can't get rid of my indigenous woman's face or my Mayan ancestry." Yet at the same time, I felt rather sad. If this sort of thing could happen to me, someone who had won the Nobel Prize, who had sent messages to the U.S. President that were published all around the world, what might not happen to the 185,000 illegal Guatemalan immigrants living in the United States?[96]

Receipt of the Nobel Prize also brought new attention to Menchú's memoir *I, Rigoberta Menchú*. The woman to whom she had dictated the story, Elisabeth Burgos, was not a part of the ceremonies celebrating Menchú's receipt of the prize. Some noted and questioned why a distance seemed to have developed between Menchú and the woman who helped publish the story that brought her such international acclaim.

At the same time, anthropologist David Stoll and others began to research the events Menchú had described in her book and discovered discrepancies between what their research revealed and what Menchú had reported in her book. Stoll noted that there was a problem with the discrepancies he was uncovering:

Rigoberta's 1982 story is not court testimony, but it is *testimonio*, an "as told to" genre that gives nonwriters, ordinarily excluded from producing literature, the chance to tell their lives in their own words. Literary scholars debate the extent to which the results should be regarded as truthful, but this is a sensitive issue. Like other such works, Rigoberta's testimonio presents itself as an eyewitness account, [and] therefore asks to be interpreted literally.[97]

Stoll's initial research pointed out inaccuracies between Menchú's account of her brother Petrocinio's death and what witnesses had told him—specifically, that Menchú and her family could not have witnessed the death, and that he was not set on fire, but instead was shot. Stoll supplied Menchú with a copy of what he had found; she quickly labeled it racist and noted to one of Stoll's colleagues, "Whites have been writing our history for five hundred years, and no white anthropologist is going to tell me what I experienced in my own flesh."[98]

CONTRADICTIONS

Additional contradictions have emerged in recent years between the account Menchú provided in *I, Rigoberta Menchú* and the story told by other witnesses and Guatemalan records. These contradictions suggest that Menchú was not uneducated and illiterate, as she had claimed, but had attended school at least up to the equivalent of middle school at two private boarding schools operated by Roman Catholic nuns, and that she was taught Spanish in these schools.

As noted earlier, additional discrepancies suggest that the land dispute that obsessed Menchú's father for most of his life was not a battle against wealthy landowners but instead was between Vicente and his in-laws. Menchú described in detail the death by starvation of her younger brother, Nicolás. Members of Menchú's own family have contradicted this story—one of her older brothers (also named Nicolás), who is 10 years older than Rigoberta, has suggested that this brother never existed.

"I had two brothers who died of hunger and disease, one named Felipe and another whose name escapes me," Nicolás Menchú told a *New York Times* reporter in 1998. "But I never knew them, because they both passed away before I was even born, and I was born in 1949."[99]

In 1998, the *New York Times* published an article that confirmed much of what David Stoll had discovered during his 10 years of research. It said,

> Relatives, neighbors, friends and former classmates of Rigoberta Menchú, including an older brother and half sister and four Roman Catholic nuns who educated and sheltered her, indicated that many of the main episodes related by Ms. Menchú have either been fabricated or seriously exaggerated.[100]

Nicolás Menchú also told the *Times* reporter that Belgian nuns, who were friends of the family, felt that Rigoberta was exceptionally bright and provided her schooling at no cost to the family. School records also confirm her attendance during the periods in question. Because of the school's schedule, it would not have been possible for Rigoberta to spend up to eight months a year working on the coffee and cotton plantations, as she claimed in *I, Rigoberta Menchú*. She also would have been in school during the period in which she claimed to have worked as an underground political organizer in her village.

UNANSWERED QUESTIONS

What are the possible reasons for the inaccuracies and discrepancies that have been discovered in Menchú's account of her life? One suggestion, advanced by Menchú herself in a September 1998 interview with the *New York Times*, is that the inaccuracies were the work of Elisabeth Burgos, who recorded and edited the tapes

Legacy of the Peacemaker

Rigoberta Menchú Tum continues to advocate for Guatemala's indigenous Mayan population. The Rigoberta Menchú Tum Foundation serves as a springboard for her activities on behalf of human rights, the rights of Guatemala's indigenous population, and ongoing efforts to achieve peace in Guatemala.

The foundation was established after Menchú received the Nobel Prize; the prize money she received provided financial support for the foundation's efforts. Its "Code of Ethics for an Era of Peace" states:

There is no Peace without Justice;

No Justice without Equality;

No Equality without Development;

No Development without Democracy;

No Democracy without Respect to the Identity and Dignity
of Cultures and Peoples.

The foundation has headquarters in Guatemala, Mexico, and the United States. Among its activities are the translation of important legal documents into K'iche', greater educational opportunities for indigenous children (including the construction of a school in Chimel), and efforts to hold those who committed atrocities against Guatemala's indigenous population legally responsible.

Menchú noted that the Mayan concept of balance plays an important role in any thoughts she has about her legacy. In *Crossing Borders,* she wrote:

I may die tomorrow, or the day after. I will not be here forever, like the eternal things on earth, but I will always be a sign of time that will remain in our Mayan memory. I am very conscious of this. A lot of people will remember me when I am dead. They'll remember the good things and the mistakes I have made, for that is how the history of humankind is made up. The attacks made on me now will be compensated for in the future.

that became the oral basis for *I, Rigoberta Menchú*: "I am the protagonist of the book, and it was my testimony, but I am not the author," she said. "She [Elisabeth Burgos] gave the book its final form, so she is officially the author of the book and has the commercial rights to it."[101]

In her 1998 memoir, *Crossing Borders*, however, Menchú clearly indicates that she was the author of *I, Rigoberta Menchú*, noting the instances where she decided to omit details or information that she felt might threaten the lives of those still in Guatemala: "I censored several parts that might have been dangerous for people. I took out bits that referred to my village, details about my brothers and sisters, and names of people."[102]

David Stoll approached Elisabeth Burgos to determine if her editing of the text could have contributed to the inaccuracies. She strongly denied this explanation, noting:

> I had to reorder a lot to give the text a thread, to give it the sense of a life, to make it a story, so that it could reach the general public, which I did via a card file, then cutting and pasting. It was hard to give it a sense of continuity in Rigoberta's own words. This is a far greater challenge than simply quoting someone as part of your own narrative. If I had wanted to do it as a professional publication, with my questions included, I could have done so, but this was not my objective.[103]

To prove her story, Burgos played several of the actual tape recordings that formed the basis of *I, Rigoberta Menchú* for Stoll. In a 1998 interview with the *New York Times*, Burgos confirmed that, "every phrase in the book comes from what Rigoberta Menchú said on the tapes." She added that she is willing to make available the tapes of the original recordings to a university for researchers to access.[104] Menchú, however, continues to dispute the criticism of her account as racist, noting that she is proud of *I, Rigoberta Menchú* as "part of the historical memory and patrimony of Guatemala."[105]

What other reasons could there be for the discrepancies in Menchú's life story? Some researchers have suggested that memory can be selective, and that the horrific events that she did experience and that happened to members of her family would be overwhelming and could result in trauma and confusion. This does not easily explain the discrepancy over her education and whether she spent much of her childhood at boarding school or working as a laborer, howerver.

Another suggestion, however, is that *I, Rigoberta Menchú* is a work of "collective memory"—she is speaking on behalf of her people, so that the experiences she described form part of the collective experience of Mayans in Guatemala.[106] This idea is supported by a phrase in the very first paragraph of *I, Rigoberta Menchú*:

> It's hard for me to remember everything that's happened to me in my life since there have been many very bad times but, yes, moments of joy as well. The important thing is that what has happened to me has happened to many other people too: My story is the story of all poor Guatemalans. My personal experience is the reality of a whole people.[107]

David Stoll suggested that, at the time she told her life story to Elisabeth Burgos, Menchú was actively involved in the revolutionary movement in Guatemala. Certain portions of her life experience—time in boarding school, a father whose land dispute was with his in-laws rather than wealthy landowners—were not necessarily in keeping with the typical oppression of Guatemalan peasants. In order to tell a story that more authentically represented the experiences of Guatemala's suffering peasants, she may have changed some of the details in her life to incorporate actual experiences that had been told to her.[108] It is possible that she did so not to make herself more important, but to make herself more truly symbolic of what her people had suffered. The story she told included events that really had taken place, even if they had not happened to her.

As details of the inaccuracies emerged in the years following Menchú's receipt of the Nobel Prize, some have suggested that the prize should be taken away from her. The Nobel Committee has firmly resisted these suggestions, pointing out that the Peace Prize was awarded to Menchú not for her writing, not for her experiences as a child, but for her ongoing work to end the oppression of her people in Guatemala and to advance the rights of all indigenous people.

Geir Lundestad, director of the Norwegian Nobel Institute, said in an interview with the *New York Times*, "All autobiographies embellish to a greater or lesser extent." He added that the decision to award the prize to Menchú was "not based exclusively or primarily on the autobiography."[109]

RECENT EVENTS

In *I, Rigoberta Menchú,* Menchú noted that the deaths of her parents had inspired her to give up any thought of marriage or motherhood. A few years after winning the Nobel Prize, however, Menchú adopted a baby boy, naming him Mash Nawalja', which means "Water Spirit." She then had a child with her companion, Angel Canil Grave. The infant, a son named Tzunun (meaning "hummingbird"), was born premature and lived for only three days. Menchú and Grave were married in 1995, and the ceremony both celebrated their marriage and marked the death of their son.

In 1995, Menchú formalized her separation from the guerilla movement by making public her dissatisfaction with the fact that the Mayans were being excluded from peace talks between the Guatemalan government and the guerillas. She removed her father's name from the organization she had founded and instead renamed it the Rigoberta Menchú Foundation, making it clear that it was not affiliated with the CUC. Many in Guatemala were equally disillusioned by the government and the guerillas, holding both groups responsible for the violence that had divided

Above, Rigoberta Menchú places a ring on the finger of her husband, Angel Canil Grave, during a ceremony to celebrate their marriage and mark the passing of Menchú's newborn son, who died after being born premature.

Guatemala for decades. Menchú wanted to make it clear that she was not affiliated with the guerilla movement, that she now represented Guatemala's indigenous population.

By 1996, Menchú had received 14 honorary doctorates, was awarded the Legion of Honor by French president Jacques Chirac, and had been appointed a goodwill ambassador of the United Nations Educational, Scientific, and Cultural Organization (UNESCO). She was on the advisory board for the New York-based Council on Foreign Relations. Although much of her human-rights campaigning had made her a figure on the international scene, by the late 1990s, she increasingly focused her appearances and activities in Guatemala. She became involved in politics, openly supporting or opposing candidates depending on their views and positions. She spoke out publicly, encouraging Guatemalans to use their political rights, to register to vote, and to vote for the candidates of their choice.

Menchú also began to advocate the idea of national unity in Guatemala, noting that there should not be the divisions and prejudices between Indians and ladinos that had contributed to the decades of war in Guatemala. Her foundation supported the Council for Mayan Education, an organization that lobbied the government to support indigenous rights, and FUNDAMAYA, an organization designed to support Mayan civic committees and Mayan-run villages.

It was while working to register voters in July 1995 that Menchú finally mustered the courage to return to Chimel. She was accompanied by her husband and a few members of her family. The village that she remembered, the home that had figured so clearly in her testimony, no longer existed. She wrote in *Crossing Borders*:

> It seemed like a different place. . . . Most of the rivers had dried up. The marshes, the swamps and the quicksands we had been so afraid of—the places where we hid for fear of snakes and mountain animals—these had all shrunk. . . . "This isn't the land I left," I said as we walked along. "Where are our mountains?" The land now belonged to landowners, and they had cut down our precious trees. Part of the hillside was bare. We remembered having played as children in the great ancient forests, and many of them had now been cut down.[110]

Menchú discovered a small community—about 24 families—living in Chimel, but they were still suffering and struggling. "The people there were so neglected and hungry that I felt sad for life itself."[111] Menchú wept for her parents and then spoke with the village's current residents. They told her of their needs, and during her next press conference, Menchú spoke of her return to her village and of the poverty still crippling people there.

Menchú returned to Chimel later, this time after spending part of the Christmas holidays with her in-laws. On December 25, 1995, she arrived late at night at Chimel in a downpour. This time, the villagers were prepared for her; there was a party with fireworks.

ADVOCATE FOR HER PEOPLE

In December 1999, Menchú filed allegations of genocide against eight of Guatemala's former dictators, presidents, and ministers in a court in Spain. Among those named, however, was the current leader of the Guatemalan Congress, Efraín Ríos Montt. A Spanish judge ruled that the Spanish court should investigate the charges.

As the investigation began, Menchú and her colleagues at the Rigoberta Menchú Foundation began to receive death threats. They were followed by suspicious cars, and their home telephones were tapped. Amnesty International reported that others who had supported Menchú's lawsuit were similarly threatened, as were several journalists whose articles were critical of the Guatemalan government.

The lawsuit charged several former Guatemalan army officers with war crimes and other human-rights violations committed between 1978 and 1986. Among the crimes with which they were charged was the assault on the Spanish embassy in 1980, in which Menchú's father was killed.

Judges and prosecutors traveled to Guatemala from Spain to interview witnesses and defendants. A leader of a Guatemalan military veterans association was quoted as saying that the judicial proceedings were "nothing more than political and legal persecution by those groups linked to the former guerrillas who want to continue the war."[112]

The case followed efforts by Menchú and others, after the signing of a peace accord between the government and guerilla groups in 1996, to ensure that those who committed war crimes during the conflict be held responsible. When this form of justice

Guatemalan president Alvaro Arzu (left) ordered Guatemalan army troops to cease hostilities against the guerrillas on March 21, 1996. The cease-fire followed the signing of a peace accord between guerrilla groups and the Guatemalan government.

was not provided by the Guatemalan legal system, the case was presented in the Spanish court. In 2006, the allegations were still under investigation by the Spanish court, and Amnesty International was in the process of calling on the Guatemalan authorities to guarantee the safety of Menchú, members of her foundation, and all those who had expressed support for the proceedings.

In a 1993 Global Vision interview, Menchú stressed that it was her belief that indigenous people should not be "protected," like an endangered species:

What we do need is simply to be allowed to exist, to live, to let our own culture develop, and to recover the meaning of our own history. Indigenous peoples have always depended on their traditional wisdom and culture. Our cosmological vision, our way of thinking, our lifestyle have empowered us to survive through many difficult times in the past. . . . The fact that indigenous people are among the most marginalised of the marginalised people on Earth, among those whose rights have been violated for so long, is a call to conscience. I hope this call will be answered."[113]

MENCHÚ'S LEGACY

Today, Rigoberta Menchú continues to work for human rights, for indigenous rights, for women's rights, and for development in Guatemala. She has become a heroine to many in Guatemala, encouraging Mayans to register to vote and to speak out against the violence and injustice they have witnessed. Her advocacy has forced her into exile several times and has resulted in death threats and fears of reprisal.

Menchú has spoken before many different groups, bringing the suffering of Guatemala's indigenous population to the attention of the world. She has spoken out about the need to fight for social change, to ensure equitable land distribution, and to protest exploitation, discrimination, and racism.

Menchú's life story, despite the criticism of its validity, shone light on the suffering of an entire group of people. It was the story of many Guatemalans—a story of injustice, of poverty, of oppression. Through its publication, the spotlight turned on Guatemala and demands for change began.

The change is slow in coming, however. As Menchú noted in *Crossing Borders*, "People have gradually got to know me. I am like a drop of water on a rock. After drip, drip, dripping in the same place, I begin to leave a mark, and I leave my mark in many people's hearts."[114]

Menchú has sought to bring about change through education and the judicial system. She has challenged those in power in

Guatemala to answer for what they did—and didn't do—during the civil war. She has exposed genocide and war crimes, and she continues to try to ensure that those who committed these crimes will answer for them. Menchú summed up her life's work in an interview published in 2000:

> There have been a lot of successes in my life. . . . And when you have success, it helps you to want to continue the struggle. You are not alone, for it's not true that it is only pain that motivates people to continue struggling to make their convictions a reality. The love of many other people, the support that one has from other people, and above all, the understanding of other people, has a lot to do with it. It's when one realizes that there are a lot of other people in the world that think the way you do, that you feel you are engaged in a larger undertaking. Every night when I go to sleep, I say a prayer that more people, more allies will support the world's struggles. That's the most important thing. That would be so good.[115]

APPENDIX

Excerpt from Rigoberta Menchú Tum's Nobel Peace Prize Acceptance Speech

This text has been translated from the original Spanish.

I feel a deep emotion and pride for the honor of having been awarded the Nobel Peace Prize. . . . I consider this Prize, not as a reward to me personally, but rather as one of the greatest conquests in the struggle for peace, for Human Rights and for the rights of the indigenous people, who, for 500 years, have been split, fragmented, as well as the victims of genocides, repression and discrimination. . . .

In my opinion, the Nobel Peace Prize calls upon us to act in accordance with what it represents, and the great significance it has worldwide. In addition to being a priceless treasure, it is an instrument with which to fight for peace, for justice, for the rights of those who suffer the abysmal economical, social, cultural and political inequalities, typical of the order of the world in which we live, and where the transformation into a new world based on the values of the human being, is the expectation of the majority of those who live on this planet. . . .

The Nobel Prize is a symbol of peace, and of the efforts to build up a real democracy. It will stimulate the civil sectors so that through a solid national unity, these may contribute to the process of negotiations that seek peace, reflecting the general feeling—although at times not possible to express because of fear—of Guatemalan society: to establish political and legal grounds that will give irreversible impulses to a solution to what initiated the internal armed conflict.

There is no doubt whatsoever that it constitutes a sign of hope in the struggle of the indigenous people in the entire Continent.

It is also a tribute to the Central-American people who are still searching for their stability, for the structuring of their future, and the path for their development and integration, based on civil democracy and mutual respect. . . .

When evaluating the overall significance of the award of the Peace Prize, I would like to say some words on behalf of all those whose voice cannot be heard or who have been repressed for having spoken their opinions, of all those who have been marginalized, who have been discriminated, who live in poverty, in need, of all those who are the victims of repression and violation of human rights. . . . The Maya people developed and spread geographically through some 300,000 square km; they occupied parts of the South of Mexico, Belize, Guatemala, as well as Honduras and El Salvador; they developed a very rich civilization in the area of political organization, as well as in social and economic fields; they were great scientists in the fields of mathematics, astronomy, agriculture, architecture and engineering; they were great artists in the fields of sculpture, painting, weaving and carving.

The Mayas discovered the zero value in mathematics, at about the same time that it was discovered in India and later passed on to the Arabs. Their astronomic forecasts based on mathematical calculations and scientific observations were amazing, and still are. They prepared a calendar more accurate than the Gregorian, and in the field of medicine they performed intracranial surgical operations. . . .

Today, it is important to emphasize the deep respect that the Maya civilization had towards life and nature in general. . . .

I would describe the meaning of this Nobel Peace prize, in the first place as a tribute to the Indian people who have been sacrificed and have disappeared because they aimed at a more dignified and just life with fraternity and understanding among human beings. To those who are no longer alive to keep up the hope for a change in the situation in respect of poverty and marginalization of the Indians, of those who have been banished, of the helpless in Guatemala as well as in the entire American Continent. . . .

Let there be freedom for the Indians, wherever they may be in the American continent or elsewhere in the world, because while they are alive, a glow of hope will be alive as well as a true concept of life.

. . . I dream of the day when the relationship between the indigenous peoples and other peoples is strengthened; when they can combine their potentialities and their capabilities and contribute to make life on this planet less unequal, a better distribution of the scientific and cultural treasures accumulated by Humanity, flourishing in peace and justice. . . .

Ladies and gentlemen, the fact that I have given preference to the American continent, and in particular to my country, does not mean that I do not have an important place in my mind and in my heart for the concern of other peoples of the world and their constant struggle in the defense of peace, of the right to a life and all its inalienable rights. The majority of us who are gathered here today, constitute an example of the above, and along these lines I would humbly extend to you my gratitude.

Many things have changed in these last years. There have been great changes of worldwide character. The East-West confrontation has ceased to exist and the Cold War has come to an end. These changes, the exact forms of which cannot yet be predicted, have left gaps that the people of the world have known how to make use of in order to come forward, struggle and win national terrain and international recognition.

Today, we must fight for a better world, without poverty, without racism, with peace in the Middle East and in Southeast Asia, to where I address a plea for the liberation of Mrs. Aung San Suu Kyi, winner of the Nobel Peace Prize 1991; for a just and peaceful solution, in the Balkans; for the end of the apartheid in South Africa; for the stability in Nicaragua, that the Peace Agreement in El Salvador be observed; for the re-establishment of democracy in Haiti; for the complete sovereignty of Panama; because all of these constitute the highest aims for justice in the international situation.

A world at peace that could provide consistency, interrelations and concordance in respect of the economic, social and cultural structures of the societies would indeed have deep roots and a robust influence.

We have in our mind the deepest felt demands of the entire human race, when we strive for peaceful co-existence and the preservation of the environment. The struggle we fight purifies and shapes the future.

Our history is a living history, that has throbbed, withstood and survived many centuries of sacrifice. Now it comes forward again with strength. The seeds, dormant for such a long time, break out today with some uncertainty, although they germinate in a world that is at present characterized by confusion and uncertainty.

There is no doubt that this process will be long and complex, but it is no Utopia and we, the Indians, we have new confidence in its implementation.

The peoples of Guatemala will mobilize and will be aware of their strength in building up a worthy future. They are preparing themselves to sow the future, to free themselves from atavisms, to rediscover their heritage. To build a country with a genuine national identity. To start a new life.

99

By combining all the shades and nuances of the "ladinos," the "garífunas" and Indians in the Guatemalan ethnic mosaic, we must interlace a number of colors without introducing contradictions, without becoming grotesque nor antagonistic, but we must give them brightness and a superior quality, just the way our weavers weave a typical huipil blouse, brilliantly composed, a gift to Humanity.

Thank you very much.

Souce: Rigoberta Menchú Tum, Nobel Lecture. Available at http://nobelprize.org/nobel-prizes/peace/laureates/1992/tum-lecture.html.

1959 Rigoberta Menchú Tum is born on January 9.

1979 Menchú's brother, Petrocinio, is kidnapped and murdered.

1980 Vicente Menchú is killed in a fire at the Spanish embassy on January 31; Juana Tum Cotojá is kidnapped on April 19, then tortured and murdered. Menchú flees to Mexico.

1981 Menchú actively works in revolutionary movement; assists Guatemalan refugees seeking exile in Mexico.

1982 Menchú travels to Paris and tells her life story to Elisabeth Burgos. Scorched earth campaign begins in Guatemala.

1983 *I, Rigoberta Menchú* is published in Spanish.

1984 New Guatemalan constitution is approved; Menchú hears portions of it read while lobbying at the United Nations.

1988 Menchú returns to Guatemala for first time, in April; is arrested and threatened with prison.

1991 Menchú participates in "500 Years Conference" in October.

1992 Menchú receives the Nobel Peace Prize.

1995 Menchú marries Angel Canil Grave; returns for the first time to Chimel.

1996 UN-sponsored agreement is signed in Guatemala; it ends more than 30 years of civil war.

1998 *Crossing Borders* is published.

1999   Menchú files allegations of genocide in Spanish court against eight former Guatemalan dictators, ministers, and presidents.

2006   Investigation of allegations of genocide continues by Spanish court; Menchú and supporters receive death threats.

Chapter 1

1. Rigoberta Menchú, *Crossing Borders*. New York: Verso, 1998, p. 14.
2. Ibid.
3. Ibid.
4. Rigoberta Menchú, *I, Rigoberta Menchú*. New York: Verso, 1984, p. 1.
5. Nobelprize.org. http://www.nobel.org.

Chapter 2

6. Menchú, *I, Rigoberta Menchú*, p. 103.
7. David Stoll, *Rigoberta Menchú and the Story of All Poor Guatemalans*. Boulder, Colo.: Westview Press, 1999, p. 27.
8. Ibid.
9. Menchú, *I, Rigoberta Menchú*, p. 32.
10. Menchú, *Crossing Borders*, p. 22
11. Ibid., p. 74.
12. Ibid., p. 90.
13. Ibid., p. 197.

Chapter 3

14. Victor Perera, *Unfinished Conquest: The Guatemala Tragedy*. Berkeley, Calif.: University of California Press, 1993, p. 2
15. Ibid., p. 6.
16. Ibid., p. 9.
17. Tom Barry, *Guatemala*. Albuquerque, N.Mex.: The Inter-Hemispheric Education Resource Center, 1989, p. 3.
18. Ibid., p. 4.

Chapter 4

19. Menchú, *Crossing Borders*, p. 45.
20. Menchú, *I, Rigoberta Menchú*, p. 21.
21. Ibid., p. 22.
22. Ibid., p. 32.
23. Ibid., p. 34.
24. Ibid.
25. Ibid., p. 35.
26. Ibid., p. 39.
27. Ibid., p. 38.
28. Ibid.
29. Ibid.
30. Ibid., p. 40.
31. Ibid., p. 41.
32. Ibid.
33. Ibid., p. 43
34. Ibid., p. 82.
35. Ibid., p. 87.
36. Ibid., pp. 88–89.
37. Ibid., p. 89.
38. Ibid.
39. Ibid., p. 90.

Chapter 5

40. Menchú, *I, Rigoberta Menchú*, p. 91.
41. Ibid., p. 111.
42. Ibid., p. 114.
43. Ibid., p. 117.
44. Ibid., p. 118.
45. Ibid., p. 122.
46. Menchú, *Crossing Borders*, p. 114.
47. Ibid., p. 114–115.
48. Menchú, *I, Rigoberta Menchú*, p. 155.
49. Ibid.
50. Ibid., p. 174.

51. Ibid., p. 178.
52. Ibid., p. 180.
53. Stoll, *Rigoberta Menchú,* p. 70.
54. Ibid., p. 87.
55. Menchú, *I, Rigoberta Menchú,* p. 184.
56. Stoll, *Rigoberta Menchú,* p. 74.
57. Ibid., p. 75.
58. Menchú, *I, Rigoberta Menchú,* p. 186.
59. Stoll, *Rigoberta Menchú,* p. 81.
60. Quoted in Stoll, *Rigoberta Menchú,* p. 82.
61. Menchú, *I, Rigoberta Menchú,* p. 200.
62. Ibid., p. 242.

Chapter 6
63. Stoll, *Rigoberta Menchú,* p. 171.
64. Menchú, *Crossing Borders,* p. 106.
65. Ibid., p. 108.
66. Ibid., p. 110.
67. Ibid., p. 113.
68. Menchú, *I, Rigoberta Menchú,* p. xiv.
69. Menchú, *Crossing Borders,* p. 114.
70. Ibid., p. 115.
71. Ibid., p. 118.
72. Ibid., p. 124.
73. Ibid., p. 125.
74. Ibid., p. 127.
75. Ibid., p. 138.

Chapter 7
76. Susanne Jonas, *The Battle for Guatemala.* Boulder, Colo.: Westview Press, 1991, p. 148.

77. Ibid., p. 149.
78. Barry, *Guatemala,* p. 10.
79. Jonas, *The Battle for Guatemala,* p. 164.
80. Ibid.
81. Menchú, *Crossing Borders,* p. 53.

Chapter 8
82. Stoll, *Rigoberta Menchú,* p. 209.
83. Ibid., p. 211.
84. Menchú, *Crossing Borders,* p. 197.
85. Quoted in Kerry Kennedy Cuomo, *Speak Truth to Power.* New York: Crown Publishers, 2000, p. 158.
86. Stoll, *Rigoberta Menchú,* p. 213.
87. Nobelprize.org. http://www.nobelprize.org.
88. Stoll, *Rigoberta Menchú,* p. 219.
89. Menchú, *Crossing Borders,* p. 19.
90. Nobelprize.org. http://www.nobelprize.org
91. Ibid.
92. Ibid.
93. Ibid.

Chapter 9
94. Menchú *Crossing Borders,* p. 192.
95. Ibid., p. 194.
96. Ibid., p. 195.
97. Stoll, *Rigoberta Menchú,* p. 226.
98. Ibid., p. 227.
99. Larry Rohter, "Tarnished Laureate," *New York Times* (December 15, 1998): pp. A1 and A8.

100. Ibid.
101. Ibid.
102. Menchú, *Crossing Borders*, p. 114.
103. Stoll, *Rigoberta Menchú,* p. 185.
104. Rohter, "Tarnished Laureate,"
     p. A8.
105. Ibid.
106. Stoll, *Rigoberta Menchú,* p. 190.
107. Menchú, *I, Rigoberta Menchú,*
     p. 1.
108. Stoll, *Rigoberta Menchú,* p. 193.
109. Rohter, "Tarnished Laureate,"
     p. A8.
110. Menchú, *Crossing Borders*, p. 199.
111. Ibid.
112. Nativo Lopez. "What's Next
     for the Immigrants Rights
     Movement?" June 30, 2006.
     Resource Center of the
     Americas. Available online.
     URL: http://www.americas.org.
113. Global Vision. Available online.
     URL: http://www.global-vision.
     org/interview/menchu.html.
114. Menchú, *Crossing Borders*,
     p. 166.
115. Cuomo, *Speak Truth to Power,*
     p. 159.

BIBLIOGRAPHY

Barry, Tom. *Guatemala*. Albuquerque, N. Mex.: The Inter-Hemispheric Education Resource Center, 1989.

Carmack, Robert M., ed. *Harvest of Violence: The Maya Indians and the Guatemalan Crisis*. Norman, Okla.: University of Oklahoma Press, 1988.

Cuomo, Kerry Kennedy. *Speak Truth to Power*. New York: Crown Publishers, 2000.

Jonas, Susanne. *The Battle for Guatemala*. Boulder, Colo.: Westview Press, 1991.

Leo, John. "Nobel Prize for Fiction?" *U.S. News and World Report* (January 25, 1999): p. 17.

Menchú, Rigoberta. *Crossing Borders*. New York: Verso Books, 1998.

Menchú, Rigoberta. *I, Rigoberta Menchú: An Indian Woman in Guatemala*. New York: Verso Books, 1984.

Perera, Victor. *Unfinished Conquest: The Guatemalan Tragedy*. Berkeley, Calif: University of California Press, 1993.

Rogachevsky, Jorge R. "David Stoll vs. Rigoberta Menchú: Indigenous Victims or Protagonists?" *Delaware Review of Latin American Studies*, Vol. 2, No. 2 (July 15, 2001).

Rohter, Larry. "Tarnished Laureate: Nobel Winner Finds Story Challenged," *New York Times* (December 15, 1998): pp. A1 and A8.

Stoll, David. *Rigoberta Menchú and the Story of All Poor Guatemalans*. Boulder, Colo.: Westview Press, 1999.

Wilkinson, Daniel. *Silence on the Mountain: Stories of Terror, Betrayal, and Forgetting in Guatemala*. Boston: Houghton Mifflin, 2002.

Zaremba, Alan. "Trouble for Rigoberta," *Newsweek* (June 21, 1999).

Web sites

Amnesty International Library
http://www.amnesty.org/library/

elPeriódico.com
http://www.elperiodico.com

Fundacion Rigoberta Menchu Tum
http://www.frmt.org

Fundación Rigoberta Menchú Tum
http://www.rigobertamenchu.org

Global Vision
http://www.global-vision.org

Indians.org
http://www.indians.org

Nobelprize.org
http://www.nobelprize.org

Quechua Network
http://www.quechuanetwork.org

Resource Center of the Americas
http://www.americas.org

The World Factbook Central Intelligence Agency
https://www.cia.gov/cia/publications/factbook/index.html

FURTHER READING

Arias, Arturo, ed. *The Rigoberta Menchú Controversy.* Minneapolis, Minn.: University of Minnesota Press, 2001.

Benz, Stephen Connely. *Guatemalan Journey.* Austin, Tex.: University of Texas Press, 1996.

Menchú, Rigoberta. *Crossing Borders.* New York: Verso Books, 1998.

Menchú, Rigoberta. *I, Rigoberta Menchú: An Indian Woman in Guatemala.* New York: Verso Books, 1984.

Sanford, Victoria. *Buried Secrets: Truth and Human Rights in Guatemala.* New York: Palgrave Macmillan, 2004.

Stoll, David. *Rigoberta Menchú and the Story of All Poor Guatemalans.* Boulder, Colo.: Westview Press, 1999.

Wilkinson, Daniel. *Silence on the Mountain: Stories of Terror, Betrayal, and Forgetting in Guatemala.* Boston: Houghton Mifflin, 2002.

Web sites

Amnesty International
http://www.amnesty.org

Nobelprize.org
http://www.nobelprize.org

United Nations: Human Rights
http://www.un.org/rights/

PICTURE CREDITS

INDEX

ABOUT THE AUTHOR

HEATHER LEHR WAGNER is a writer and editor. She is the author of more than 30 books exploring social and political issues and focusing on the lives of prominent men and women. She earned a B.A. in political science from Duke University and an M.A. in government from the College of William and Mary. She lives with her husband and family in Pennsylvania. She is the author of *Henry Kissinger, Elie Wiesel,* and *Anwar Sadat and Menachem Begin* in the MODERN PEACEMAKERS series.